GETTING RID OF
THE GORILLA

GETTING RID OF
THE GORILLA

CONFESSIONS ON THE STRUGGLE TO FORGIVE

BRIAN JONES

Standard®
PUBLISHING
Bringing The Word to Life

Cincinnati, Ohio

Published by Standard Publishing, Cincinnati, Ohio
www.standardpub.com

Also available: *Getting Rid of the Gorilla Group Member Discussion Guide*
ISBN 978-0-7847-2163-6

Printed in USA
Project editor: Diane Stortz
Cover and interior design: The DesignWorks Group

ISBN 978-0-7847-2152-0

Library of Congress Cataloging-in-Publication Data

Jones, Brian, 1967-
    Getting rid of the gorilla : confessions on the struggle to forgive / Brian Jones.
        p. cm.
    ISBN 978-0-7847-2152-0 (soft cover)
    1. Forgiveness—Religious aspects—Christianity. 2. Forgiveness of sin. I. Title.

BV4647.F55J66 2008
241'.4—dc22

                                        2007042701

14 13 12 11 10 09 08   9 8 7 6 5 4 3 2 1

DEDICATION

FOR GRANDMA JONES

The last time I saw you in the hospital, I told you that you needed to believe that God was going to make you better. I kept insisting, "You've got to believe, Grandma. You've got to believe." Sensing my fear, you smiled, put your hand on my cheek, and said, "Say, how about I just believe in you." One of the reasons I can't wait to get to heaven is to see you again.

A WORD ABOUT GORILLAS

The metaphor of a gorilla for an unforgiving heart is purely a literary tool. The only gorillas we want to get rid of are the ones in our hearts. If you would like to support the conservation of gorillas and their habitats in Africa through antipoaching patrols, regular monitoring, research, education, and support of local communities, please see www.gorillafund.org.

CONTENTS

1   ORIGINS   9

TRACKING THE GORILLA

2   RAGE   21

3   DISTANCE   31

4   PESSIMISM   57

GORILLA DNA

5   MYTHS   69

6   BELIAL   83

GETTING RID OF THE GORILLA

7   CALL   103

8   KINDNESS   115

9   PRAYER   135

10   MIRROR   153

11   SHEPHERDS   175

12   JOY   187

I
ORIGINS

In the Bible, Jesus taught that if we don't forgive the people who hurt us in this life, there's a pretty good chance God won't forgive us in the next. What scares me about this is not so much what might happen to me if I don't forgive, but that most of the time I don't really seem to care.

Don't get me wrong. I don't want to go to hell any more than the next guy (especially if eternal conscious torment ends up involving some form of nonstop Barry Manilow music marathon). It's just that the threat of hell doesn't move me any longer.

I want to say I got this way because I've been so wounded in the past that I already feel like I've been through hell—but that would be a lie. I've been hurt, deeply at times, but nothing like what some family members and friends have experienced. To say I've been through hell would cheapen their memories, their stories, and their pain.

Another part of me wants to blame God himself for how I feel about this. I want to be able to tell people that Jesus' threat of judgment doesn't move me because I've become more moral than God. The way I see it, if God *allowed* me to be hurt even though he could have stopped it, and now demands that I forgive the ones who hurt me and makes *his* forgiveness dependent upon mine—maybe he's not the kind of God I thought he was. Maybe he's the last person I want to hang out with. Maybe not spending eternity with a God like that is a pretty good option. I may think like this at times, but if I tell you that God is the root of my dilemma, I will be less than honest.

I know this will probably come as quite a shock to you, but I believe the reason I've become indifferent toward Jesus' warning is that *I don't like forgiving people*. It's that simple. I just don't like forgiving people. And what is really sad is that I'm fairly certain I wasn't born this way; in fact, I know I wasn't. I don't think any of us are born this way. Most sins we struggle with are sins we choose, but an unforgiving heart begins, I believe, when pain chooses us. And I know the exact day, time, and place it happened: seventh grade, Orton Davis Park, behind the snack shack, about twenty-five yards from the tennis courts.

I was watching a friend play a youth league football game, and then, without knowing exactly what happened, I found myself surrounded by a crowd of high school dropouts who had recently formed a gang called The Cornered Rats. With nothing but time on their hands, they spent their days smashing mailboxes, shoplifting from supermarkets, and breaking into cars. (No one really took them seriously until an elderly man was shot in the chest with a sawed-off shotgun.) Somehow they stumbled upon me at the football game, and for the next ten minutes I was their entertainment.

After the melee of kicks and punches subsided, I somehow managed to stand up and catch a good-enough glimpse of the ringleader to file a police report. Eight weeks later, we were all sitting together in court, me on the witness stand, the judge to my right, and the ringleader's lawyer in front of me, asking penetrating questions.

After repeated attempts to get me to contradict myself, the lawyer pointed to me and said, "You're a big boy. I want you to show the judge and everyone here what my client did to you." Then he put his arms to his side and snidely said, "Go ahead. I'm your punching bag. Take a swing."

I didn't know what to do. My assailant's last punch had knocked me almost unconscious. Since I was sure the police report should have sufficed to describe what happened, I raised my right hand, trembling, fearful that I would hurt him, and politely nudged the lawyer's stomach.

"That's why you're prosecuting my client?" he yelled in front of everyone.

Then the guy who hit me laughed. He leaned forward, pounded his palms on the table in front of him, and howled with laughter.

I sat down, looked at the floor, and helplessly boiled over with rage. Like the main character, Mersault, in Albert Camus's book *The Stranger*, "blind rage had washed me clean, rid me of hope; for the first time, in that night alive with signs and stars, I opened myself to the gentle indifference of the world."[1]

Today I have to close my eyes and think long and hard to recall the face of my attacker. But his laugh . . . that's another thing.

A friend who was sexually abused by her uncle at age four says it's the smell of his cologne she can't forget.

For another friend, it's the texture of the crumpled love note she discovered in the pocket of her husband's laptop bag.

First Corinthians 13:5 says that love "keeps no record of wrongs." The best I can tell, the wrongs themselves aren't what we catalog and keep recalling. It's the triggers, the ambient sounds and sensations that bring back the feelings of rage. These are what we can't help recording and what keep us from forgetting the wrongs done to us.

That was the day an unforgiving heart chose me, and my guess is that you can remember the exact day, time, and circumstances it happened to you as well.

The morning after the trial, when I woke up and pushed the covers back, someone was standing at the side of my bed, staring at me. He wasn't visible, but I could feel his presence nonetheless, the embodiment of a strange mix of emotions I had never felt before. He followed me to school, sat next to me during class, and walked one step behind me all the way home again.

For some reason, rather than chase him away, I continued to feed him throughout the day, adding the pain and negative energy of the last few months, connecting the dots between the rage I felt at the trial and other recent, painful, poignant hurts. The more I rolled the emotions I was feeling over and around, like a little kid making a snowman in the backyard, the more my anger, memory, and vengeful resolve began to grow and meld into something with a life and shape of its own. From that day forward, my life has never been the same.

A GIGANTIC METAPHOR

I'll never forget taking my kids to a small zoo in Florida and standing in the middle of the primate section, surrounded by cages full of orangutans, baboons, and chimpanzees. The smaller monkeys entertained everyone by swinging on ropes and scaling the bars of the cage, but what kept me mesmerized was the huge gorilla sitting in front of me. For some odd reason, he kept staring at me. So I stared back. I made a face, and he looked away. He made a sound, and I moved side to side, waving my arms in the air like I was guarding a basketball player. This went on for about ten minutes until my wife walked over. "Look at this gorilla," I said. "I think I'm really making a connection with him. I mean, I say something and then he—"

THUD.

Something bounced off my shoe. The gorilla just sat there, rocking back and forth, staring the other direction. I looked down and couldn't believe my eyes: gorilla poop all over my new sneakers! Before I could look up again, something went flying by my head. Then something nicked my shorts.

"This stupid ape is throwing poop at me!" I screamed. "You stupid animal, look at me when I'm—"

CLUNK.

Another piece of poop went whizzing by, then another and another. Finally I ran up to the cage, screaming at the gorilla, and he roared back at me. The two of us must have made quite a commotion, because within seconds a zookeeper ran over to me and said, "I wouldn't do that if I were you."

"Why not? What's he going to do? In case you haven't noticed, I'm out here and he's behind those steel bars!"

The zookeeper shook his head. "He's so strong he could rip that cage door off with one arm if he wanted to. The only reason he's in there is because he doesn't know he can get out."

That moment marked me, and not because of the poop on my shoes. I had finally found a metaphor that helped me understand what happened to me on the witness stand when I was thirteen. Unbeknownst to me, while my family and I drove home from court, someone else was headed toward my house as well. I've been struggling to figure out how to uninvite him from my life ever since.

Living with an unforgiving heart is like living with a gorilla. I don't mean trekking on safari to see gorillas in the wild, trying to fit into their environment with the least disturbance possible. I mean trying to go about your daily routine while one of their slightly overweight cousins sits on your family room couch, playing with the remote control. I'm thinking of the kind that used to travel with the circus and bum cigarettes off people in grocery store parking lots. I mean the gorilla that beats his chest when you run out of ice cream and blasts holes in your drywall like a construction worker's wrecking ball, a gorilla strong enough to kill you but domesticated enough to sit down with you and your kids on the living room floor and eat pepperoni pizza and chug seventeen cans of root beer. A gorilla that doesn't know he can leave because you've never told him, a gorilla you can get used to having around if you're desperate enough. That's what it's like to live with an unforgiving heart.

The primary Greek word for the word Jesus used for *forgiveness* is *aphiemi*, formed by the combination *apo*, meaning "from," and *hiemi,* meaning "to send." *Aphiemi* is used 142 times in the New Testament, and most of those uses describe actions *other than* forgiveness. For instance, Mark 1:34 says, "And Jesus healed many who had various diseases. He also drove out [*aphiemi*] many demons." But in the 45 instances where *aphiemi* is used to describe the act of forgiveness, it still retains the sense of releasing something closely held or trapped.[2]

Notice how the verses below take on new meaning when *aphiemi* is translated *release* instead of *forgive.*

> *Release* our debts, as we also have *released* our debtors (Matthew 6:12).

> For if you *release* men when they sin against you, your heavenly Father will also *release* you. But if you do not *release* men [from] their sins, your Father will not *release* your sins (Matthew 6:14, 15).

> The servant's master took pity on him, *released* the debt and let him go (Matthew 18:27).

> This is how my heavenly Father will treat each of you unless you *release* your brother from your heart (Matthew 18:35).

> And when you stand praying, if you hold anything against anyone, *release* him, so that your Father in heaven may *release* you [from] your sins (Mark 11:25, 26).

According to Jesus, regardless of the magnitude of the hurts we receive at the hands of others, if we don't find a way to release and pardon the people who hurt us, our pain and anger settle at the bottom of our souls. Then without our knowing it, they find each other and begin to grow. Over time the rage and tears of other hurts are added, and the sum of the parts takes on a life of its own. What we're forced to deal with is no longer one isolated incident but all of them together. The gorilla came to live with us the moment we chose not to forgive. Now he's larger, more powerful—overwhelming.

The illusion is that over time we can isolate the gorilla, domesticate him and cage him and get on with our lives, but that's an impossible task. Living with the gorilla changes everything about us. Nothing in our lives goes untouched. The gorilla can't be tucked away in a corner closet in the basement of our lives. Just when we think we're free from his tantrums, just when we think we've soothed him enough to sit still and watch a video, he kicks over the television and scares everyone away. The gorilla ruins marriages. He ruins friendships. He growls at family gatherings and beats his chest at church. An unforgiving heart affects everyone and everything we touch.

The first time I really understood this was soon after our second child was born. My wife received a phone call from a near stranger— her father. He had received one of our Christmas cards with a family photo and, true to form, made his obligatory every-three-years phone call to see how things were going. "I'd like to meet my granddaughters over Christmas if it's OK with you," he told Lisa, inviting our entire family to his home.

Hearing Lisa start making plans over the phone, I waved my hands back and forth and yelled in the background, "There is no way I'm letting that man around my daughters!" But convinced of her need to try to put the past behind her, at least so our daughters could know their grandfather, Lisa agreed to go. She hung up the phone and I immediately said, "You're going without me."

Three weeks later, after much wrangling on my part, we stood on her father's doorstep—Lisa, our daughters, me . . . and the gorilla. I leaned over to Lisa and said, "Thirty minutes and we're gone."

To my surprise, Lisa's father and his wife were as polite and kind as could be. They had bought Christmas gifts for the kids and prepared a wonderful Christmas dinner. I could tell that her father was really trying to make a connection with Lisa—commenting on how beautiful she looked and how much she seemed to enjoy being a mother. I was impressed by how much patience he had with our kids and the way he seemed to really want to be a part of their lives. It could have been a real turning point for him, for Lisa, for our girls, and even for me, but I was not about to let that happen.

Every time he asked me a question, I shot back a short, sarcastic response. I crossed my arms and stared at him the way a security guard stares at a homeless person entering a high-end clothing store. I tried every which way I could to let him know that I hated him for what he put my wife through. I barked and charged and kicked and beat my chest, all the tricks I had learned from living with the gorilla.

But Lisa's father didn't respond in kind like I thought he would. After a while, he and his wife took the girls to his den to show them something he made them for Christmas. Lisa turned to me and said, "Stop it. Just stop it."

"I am not about to sit here and pretend that the first eighteen years of your life didn't happen," I said. "I've got something he wants, his grandchildren, and you'd better be sure I'm going to make him pay."

Then Lisa looked at me and said something that to this day still makes me emotional. She said, "Brian, this is all I've got. This is all he's capable of. Please let this happen."

And that was the moment I realized I had to stop. I looked at my daughter walking down the steps with her grandfather, I saw the smile on her face and the hope in his eyes, and I knew that the time had come. The gorilla I tried to keep a hidden houseguest for twenty-five years had worn out his welcome. My unforgiving heart was no longer affecting just me; it was beginning to affect my wife and children too.

I had thought I could domesticate the gorilla and keep him safely tucked away, but I couldn't. And once I realized that, I knew I had a choice to make. I had to get rid of the gorilla.

This book is the story of how I've struggled to do that and what I've learned along the way.

TRACKING THE GORILLA

2
RAGE

The evangelicalism I grew up in . . . only allowed us to express a very narrow band of emotions: joy, certainly, but anger, never. . . . If you weren't joyful all the time, you weren't a real Christian.

—GORDON MACDONALD

I've been going to a therapist off and on now for about two years. Not a counselor, a massage therapist. My friend Andy, one of those New Age hippy types, works at the local mall giving chair massages.

The first time I got a massage, I thought I was on a reality TV show. Andy leaned over as he was rubbing my shoulders and whispered, "Dude, you've got great celestial aura."

"Thanks," I said. "I hear that a lot."

A few years ago, I made a deal with myself. My insurance co-payment is twenty dollars per doctor's office visit. I decided that, if at the end of the month I hadn't gotten sick, I'd use my budgeted co-payment money to go see Andy for some good old-fashioned stress relief while my wife and daughters go shopping. Since I haven't been to the doctor in over two years, Andy and I have developed a nice friendship.

The other day when I sat down in the massage chair, Andy started out by brushing his hands up and down my back five or six times, like he was sweeping away mosquitoes. (I learned early on that he does this to cleanse my aura of negative energy.)

"Now breathe through your nose for fifteen seconds, taking in all the sounds around you," Andy told me. "OK, now hold it in for ten. When you exhale, picture yourself releasing all the toxic energy in your body, bringing your celestial craniosacral fluids into spiritual alignment."

Inwardly I laugh every time he does this. Andy knows I'm a pastor and hope to introduce him to Jesus someday, but in the meantime there's just something comical about an evangelical pastor developing a genuine friendship with a guy who drinks seaweed shakes and spends his weekends doing yoga at Hindu ashrams.

"So why are you here today?" Andy asked.

"I threw my back out playing softball with my daughter."

"No, you didn't. Your body is in communication with the celestial world. Your natural mind is interpreting that as back pain, but really it's a signal that you are out of harmony with your higher self."

"Either that or I just threw my back out."

"Oh, really?" Andy asked sternly. "Then why are you here?"

"Like I said, I threw my back out."

"I hear that, Brian, but why are you here? You keep coming back month after month to get rid of something."

"Stress?"

"Deeper than that," he said as he pushed with both hands on my lower back. "What's the one unresolved problem that never leaves you?"

A word instantly came to my mind, but I didn't want to say it. I felt strange. Strange in the sense that I should be the one asking the spiritual questions, not him—I'm the one who understands real truth, biblical truth, not the pagan swami stuff that Andy quotes to me. Strange in the sense that I felt the presence of the Holy Spirit right there in the middle of the mall. Strange because for some reason I felt like opening up about what I was thinking.

"You really want to know?"

"Yeah."

"Anger. I can't remember a time in my life when I haven't been angry."

Suddenly Andy stopped pressing on my shoulders, pulled his hands back, and asked me one of the most profound spiritual questions I've ever been asked.

"Why are you so angry?"

WHY ARE YOU SO ANGRY?

Has anyone ever asked you that question? Whether we like to admit it or not, those of us who struggle with an unforgiving heart also carry around a tremendous amount of anger. Anger and an unforgiving heart always go hand in hand. Have you ever asked yourself Andy's question? As I've wrestled with my anger through the years and looked to Scripture for insight about my experience, I noticed that the Bible doesn't just talk about anger all by itself; it talks about anger *and* rage.

Over time, I began to realize that maybe the one unresolved problem that never left me wasn't anger at all; maybe it was something much deeper, much more troubling. I began to realize that what I shared with Andy was the correct emotion, but the wrong name. What I struggle with is what the Bible calls rage. If you struggle with an unforgiving heart, my guess is that rage could be your real struggle too. What I would like to do is share one of the most helpful things someone in our predicament can come to understand to kick-start the forgiveness process—the difference between anger and rage.

ANGER: A NORMAL, PROPORTIONATE RESPONSE

Anger is a normal and proportionate response to being hurt.

What I mean by proportionate is that the anger we feel almost always matches in kind the severity of the pain inflicted on us. If someone says something that hurts us, we get angry, but usually that anger is proportionate; we respond in kind. We want to say something hurtful back, or we yell, or we secretly pray that God will allow the other person to eat a spoiled egg-salad sandwich or something. Our initial emotional response is equal to the violation. We don't grab a baseball bat to break the legs of the person who's been mean to us. That would be a disproportionate response. It doesn't fit the violation.

Likewise, if someone lures our sister into a dark alley and brutally violates and murders her, our natural, unfiltered response is proportionate then too: we want to kill the perpetrator. The violation is so severe and so damaging that everything within us wants to respond in kind. The deep sense of shock and violation we feel enrages us and causes us to want to react proportionately. Anger is always an emotion that reacts proportionately—small violations illicit small responses, medium violations illicit medium responses, and life-altering violations illicit life-altering responses.

Anger is also a normal response to being hurt. It's normal to be angry when someone is unkind to you. It's normal to want to kill someone for killing your loved one. Both responses are normal reactions. The Bible tells us, "In your anger do not sin" (Ephesians 4:26). Anger is not a sin. Anger is a feeling, an emotion. Anger is not a sign of unformed Christian character. It is not a sign that you have some spiritual growing up to do. Feeling angry when you've been hurt is not a sign of weakness; it's a sign that you have a pulse.

The original Greek word the Bible uses for *anger* is *orge*, which means to "be puffed up, swell" or "be excited."[1] Anger is a normal, God-given emotion. It causes us to protect ourselves. Numerous passages in the Bible seem to condemn anger, but what they're really condemning is the behavior we display when we act on our anger, not the initial feeling of anger itself. Despite what well-meaning Christians might have told you in the past, there is something severely wrong with you if you don't feel angry when you are hurt.

RAGE: AN ABNORMAL, DISPROPORTIONATE RESPONSE

Rage, on the other hand, is an abnormal and disproportionate response to being hurt.

Rage exceeds the severity of the violation we experience. Someone says an unkind word to us, and we respond by punching him in the face. Someone cuts us off accidentally in traffic, and we floor it and chase after her for six miles down the turnpike. Someone interrupts us while we're trying to concentrate on a report at work, and we "fly off the handle" and throw the papers in the air. There is definitely something wrong and sinful about rage.

Rage is one of the best ways to know whether we've been spending too much time with the gorilla. In her classic book *Gorillas in the Mist*, researcher and preservationist Dian Fossey uses words like *dignified* and *gentle* to describe the natural behavior of the gorillas she studied.[2] Yet she also describes how, on rare occasions, a gorilla might beat its chest and charge after her in a horrifying fit of terror if she simply came into its territory or looked it in the eyes.[3] Rage is like that—a calm veneer one second, explosive behavior the next.

Rage is much more than a physical response, however. Some of the most rage-filled people I know never raise their voices. That's because rage is a continuous state of internal bitterness. Rage is anger that has overstayed its welcome, anger that is no longer directed toward one person in particular. We know we're struggling with rage when we've moved from being angry *at someone* to just being angry. Rage is not the emotional result of going to bed one night having failed to resolve what made us angry that day; rage is a decade of going to bed with unresolved anger, allowing it to congeal and harden in our soul.

When we respond disproportionately, we're allowing a trigger—something completely unrelated to our years of emotional hemorrhaging—to cause us to spew outside ourselves what's been festering internally. That's why I don't find it coincidental that the Greek word for *rage* in the Bible is *thymos*, which means "to boil up."[4] A random, rage-filled response simply gives the outside world a glimpse into what's been percolating inside of us for years.

Most important, rage is an abnormal response. Not just because commonly accepted rules of social etiquette frown upon punching your golf partner in the gut when he laughs at your bad putt, but because rage is toxic. I hate being consumed with rage; I hate being angry all the time. But do you want to know what I hate even more? I hate the fact that I've never known a time when I wasn't angry; I hate knowing that someone else had some part in making me this way. I'm angry because someone changed me and left me to clean up the mess. I'm angry that I'm angry.

MAKING A CHOICE

My guess is that because you picked up this book, you're angry too. Someone gossiped about you. Someone betrayed you. Someone cheated on you. Someone lied to you. Someone abused you. Someone did something to you that you can't forget, and deep inside you've been carrying around this thing that you can't seem to get rid of, and it's just become too much. Like me, you're filled with rage, and even though you've probably never admitted it to anyone, you've been this way for a very long time.

We couldn't help getting angry when we were hurt; we had no choice in the matter. We can, however, make a decision about whether we'll allow that anger to turn into rage. That is a decision we do have control over. Anger is something that happens naturally; rage is something that we help manufacture.

If you're like me, the decision to live with rage rather than to forgive the people who hurt you seemed like the better option at the time. But I think you would agree that the more you've lived with rage, the more you've regretted that decision. The person you have hurt most has been the person staring back at you in the mirror. Frederick Buechner wrote: "Of the Seven Deadly Sins, anger is possibly the most fun. To lick your wounds, to smack your lips over grievances long past, to roll over your tongue the prospect of bitter confrontations still to come, to savor to the last toothsome morsel both the pain you are given and the pain you are giving back—in many ways it is a feast fit for a king. The chief drawback is that what you are wolfing down is yourself. The skeleton at the feast is you."[5]

The great thing about Christianity is that no decision is ever final. There's still time to make a change. We don't have to live with rage for the rest of our lives. Ephesians 4:31, 32 tells us, "Get rid of all bitterness, rage and anger, brawling and slander, along with every form of malice. Be kind and compassionate to one another, forgiving each other, just as in Christ God forgave you." There's still time for us to get rid of our rage and allow forgiveness to happen.

A few years ago, I was preparing for a sermon on the story of the woman caught in adultery, found in the Gospel of John. Since it's a well-known passage, even among nonchurchgoing types, I really struggled with how to make it come alive. Finally, after weeks of sermon-writer's block, I had an idea. My team and I purchased hundreds of rocks from a local landscaping company and had our ushers hand them out to people as they walked into the service.

Nothing was said from the stage to explain why people were given the rocks, but as I began to teach on the passage, everyone quickly caught on. I talked at length about how just as the crowd picked up rocks to stone the woman in John's account, the rocks we were holding represented the anger we harbored toward someone who had harmed each of us in some way.

Despite our right to be angry with those who had hurt us, the time had come to move on. Just as those who stood before the woman caught in adultery dropped their rocks and walked away, it was time for us to encounter Jesus and do the same. It was time to follow the way of Jesus and forgive. It was time for us to drop our rocks.

"Here's what we're going to do," I said. "Today we're going to celebrate the Lord's Supper together, but instead of the ushers passing the trays to you where you're seated, we're all going to walk up here and drop our rocks into buckets across the front of the room, symbolizing our willingness to forgive whoever has hurt us. Once you've done that, take an individual piece of bread and a cup and then walk back to your seat."

No one moved, so I went first and dropped my rock. As I let it fall from my fingers, I told God that I was finally choosing to forgive someone who had spent a great deal of energy slandering me. After me came a teenager; I turned to her and smiled. She mustered a polite half smile in return, choking back tears. After her another person slowly came forward, and then another, and finally the entire congregation was walking toward the front of the auditorium.

I still remember the clanging of those rocks, a strange clashing of sounds as one rock after another dropped into the buckets. Some people dropped their rocks politely; others threw them down with the force of a running back spiking a football after a touchdown. Others lingered in front of the buckets, blocking the line of people behind them, unsure of whether they could let their rocks go.

More than a year later, an elderly woman in our congregation approached one of our staff members in the hallway between services. Reaching into her purse, she said, "I've finally reached a point where I'm ready to forgive my father for what he did to me growing up." And then she pulled out one of the rocks from that service, gently placed it in his hand, and said, "I've been carrying this rock for too long. I'd like to put it down now."

There's still time for you to do the same.

3
DISTANCE

I imagine that one of the reasons people cling to their hates
so stubbornly is because they sense, once hate is gone, that
they will be forced to deal with pain.

—James Baldwin

I have a really hard time talking about the subject of this chapter, so I thought that maybe the best way to ease into the discussion is to share a short children's story that I wrote. I'm not too sure I'll ever read it to my kids, but maybe I should someday . . .

Once upon a time there was a happy boy named Brian.

He loved the people in his life.

But as he grew up, he discovered
that people could be mean . . .

... and that he could be just as mean in return.

So he took a tiny step away
from those around him.

And another.

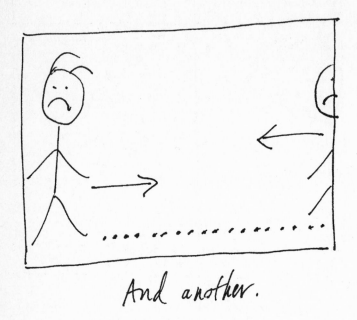

And another.

until he knew he was far enough away
that no one would ever be able to hurt
him again.

When Brian grew up, he continued
to keep people at arm's length.

He was much happier
living life this way.

At least that's what he
kept telling himself.

A STRUGGLE WITH INTIMACY

I struggle with intimacy. As long as I can remember, I've felt an oppositional push away from people, much like the invisible force you feel when you try to push the negative (or positive) ends of two magnets together. Every self-help book, every psychologist, anyone who's studied emotional health will tell you that lack of intimacy is a really dangerous thing. Just knowing this is so creates as much shame as the struggle itself!

I'm extremely guarded and protective. It takes a very long time for relationships to unfold for me; trust is a huge issue. I struggle with letting people get close; I struggle even more with wanting to let them get close in the first place. I fight to allow people to get past the subtle defense mechanisms that I've worked for years to master. Outside of my family, I can count on one hand the number of people I've allowed to get close enough to get to know the real me.

Part of my problem stems from my temperament (I'm an introvert), and I'm sure part of it stems from my upbringing. My gut tells me, however, that the primary reason I struggle with intimacy comes from my long struggle with an unforgiving heart. I remember counseling someone, "You show me a person who wrestles with an unforgiving heart, and I'll show you someone who struggles with intimacy." The person I was speaking to had no idea that I knew this to be true because I was really talking about myself.

Intimacy is a topic usually reserved for books on marriage, but I think it belongs more in a discussion about forgiveness. Our English word *intimacy* comes from the Latin word *intimus*, which means "within."[1] *Intimus* is an adjective in the superlative form. If you didn't fall asleep in your high school grammar class like I did, you probably remember that there are three kinds of adjectives: positive, comparative, and superlative. *Intimate* is the positive form of the adjective. *More intimate* is the comparative form. *Most intimate* is the superlative form. Likewise, the Latin adjective *intimus* doesn't mean just "within" or "more within"; it means "the most within." It's the most within something you can go.

That's my problem—letting people into that place most within myself where I'm vulnerable and defenseless. The macho, manly part of me hesitates to admit this, for fear you'll think I struggle with erectile dysfunction or something. That's not my struggle; my difficulty is much more debilitating than that. What I struggle with is not an inhibited sex life, or being unfriendly, or lacking lots of casual friends, or even being unable to talk about deeply personal things. What I find difficult is sustaining long-term "behind the curtain" relationships with people who want a backstage pass to see me when I'm unfiltered and raw.

If you struggle with forgiveness, chances are good you know exactly what I'm talking about.

It's important to point out, however, that it's natural to create distance between ourselves and people who hurt us. How else would we be expected to respond to someone who rummages through our trash and steals our identity—go out on a date afterward? Proverbs 4:23 cautions us, "Above all else, guard your heart, for it is the wellspring of life." Our heart is that most sensitive part of who we are. It's that place deep inside us where we feel a bomb go off when we hear things like "I don't love you anymore" or "I'm sorry, but your position has been eliminated." No one has to explain the importance of guarding our hearts to someone who has been wounded.

GUARDING OUR HEARTS

The writer of Proverbs understood how crucial it is to guard the spiritual and emotional core of who we are. Notice the phrase "above all else." There was no punctuation in ancient Hebrew, so to call attention to something he wanted to emphasize, a Jewish writer placed it at the beginning of the sentence. By placing "above all else" at the front of this proverb, the writer was saying, "Trust me, whatever you do in life, and I mean whatever you do, make sure you guard your heart!"

In 1997 I learned why this is important. That was the year I quit being a pastor. I didn't make a formal announcement to my congregation, but I might as well have; I was out of there. In my mind I had one very good reason for removing my hand from the plow: a man I'll call Jim.

He was an older gentleman who felt called by God to be my accountability partner—without asking me. One day he offered to take me out to eat, and, underprepared for what was about to happen, I accepted. Setting down his sandwich, Jim said, "Brian, there are hundreds of things you are doing wrong at our church, but for the sake of time I've shortened my list to ten."

Caught completely off guard, I made the mistake of saying, "Start with number one." Two and a half hours later, I left with 50 percent less self-esteem and a really good case for why first cousins should never marry.

After that meeting, Jim decided it was his special calling from God to point out my mistakes on a weekly basis—through letters, phone calls, notes in the offerings bowls, frowns during my sermons, and endless discussions with other church members behind my back. Jim was the first person I ever met with the spiritual gift of slander. In his book *Travels with Charley*, John Steinbeck remarked, "Strange how one person can saturate a room with vitality, with excitement. Then there are others . . . who can drain off energy and joy, can suck pleasure dry and get no sustenance from it. Such people spread a grayness in the air about them."[2] That was Jim, and I hated him for it. For an entire year, he wrecked my life—he single-handedly wrecked me emotionally.

There's a reason Proverbs 4:23 cautions us to guard our hearts: God doesn't expect us to keep allowing people like Jim to hurt us. God isn't sadistic; he doesn't expect us to keep going back for second helpings of pain. Creating distance is simply a way we guard our hearts from getting trampled on again and again.

In my experience, there are two kinds of distance we tend to create between ourselves and those who hurt us: geographical and emotional.

Geographical Distance

Recently a young man grabbed me by the arm in the hallway before church. I was in a hurry, literally seconds away from going up to the stage to speak, but I could tell he was distraught, so I stopped.

"I caught her again," he said. Holding a baby in one arm, he used the heel of his other hand to wipe away tears from his eyes. "She said she was sorry, but this is the fourth time she's done this. I've had enough. I kicked her out."

My heart sank. I was heartbroken for him and enraged at her at the same time, but before I could hug him or pray or do anything, an usher came up and said, "You're on."

As I walked to the podium and began to talk, I could see my friend sit down in the far right-hand corner of the auditorium. Soon I was deeply engrossed in my message. Halfway through, however, much to my absolute disbelief, I saw his wife casually walk in, sneaking in the back door and squeezing past people to find a seat right beside her husband. I tried to concentrate and regain my train of thought.

Throughout the rest of my sermon, I occasionally looked toward the two of them—him staring straight ahead in a daze, her staring down at the floor. But as I began to wrap up, I noticed that something dramatic had happened: there was a seat in between the two of them. Sometime during the last half of my sermon, without fanfare, my friend had picked up his infant daughter and moved over one seat. It was a simple shift, but it communicated volumes to his wife and even to my friend himself.

That little action represents the first kind of distance we create in our relationships when we're hurt: geographical distance. Sometimes it's moving an entire state away that helps. Sometimes it's just a zip code. Sometimes it's across the street or into another room. Sometimes it's just a seat away.

Distancing ourselves geographically allows us space to regroup and heal. It protects us from even more anguish. Maybe you've had to ask your spouse to leave the house. Maybe you had to quit a job you loved because you worked for a boss you hated. Maybe you had to move away from your parents. I once knew someone who joined the military because he couldn't think of another way to create enough distance between himself and his alcoholic father's beatings.

I've always found the verbal fistfight between Paul and Barnabas in Acts 15:36-41 instructive:

> Some time later Paul said to Barnabas, "Let us go back and visit the brothers in all the towns where we preached the word of the Lord and see how they are doing." Barnabas wanted to take John, also called Mark, with them, but Paul did not think it wise to take him, because he had deserted them in Pamphylia and had not continued with them in the work. They had such a sharp disagreement that they parted company. Barnabas took Mark and sailed for Cyprus, but Paul chose Silas and left, commended by the brothers to the grace of the Lord. He went through Syria and Cilicia, strengthening the churches.

One thing that jumps out at me when I read that passage is how the apostle Paul struggled with relationships just like you and me. Paul felt so wounded by Mark's betrayal that he simply couldn't stand being around him anymore; Mark's presence was toxic. Paul didn't try to joke about it and smooth it over. He didn't sweep it under the rug. He didn't overspiritualize it. He was honest with himself, Barnabas, John Mark, and everyone around them, and we're given no indication that "the sharp disagreement" he instigated was considered sinful in any way.

The other thing that stands out is the two phrases "Mark . . . sailed for Cyprus" and "He [Paul] went through Syria and Cilicia."

I wonder if sometimes the only way to move past a traumatic event and heal is to put a literal ocean between our hearts and the people who hurt us.

EMOTIONAL DISTANCE

When our children were small, all the neighborhood kids would come over to our house to play in our basement. While they liked the dress-up clothes, the videos, and all the other toys we had, their attention always turned to the large plastic playhouse in the corner. Big enough for six or seven children to fit inside, it was the perfect hideout. Just about every day, it seemed, the children formed a new secret club and used the playhouse as their base of operations.

One afternoon I went downstairs and noticed a 5 x 8 index card taped to the door of the playhouse. I recognized my oldest daughter's handwriting. I pictured Kelsey, always a natural leader, gathering her club members together and telling them that in order to be successful they needed to establish ground rules for how they were going to operate. Here, unedited, is what my daughter had written:

RULES

1. NO PUSHING
2. NO YELLING
3. NO Fighting
4. NO Argueing
5. No tatel taleing
6. NO hideing bad papers!!!!
7. No burping

8. No stink Bombs

9. No hiting

10. DO YOUR BEST

I still laugh when I read the list. No pushing, yelling, fighting, or arguing all are really good rules. I'm sure rule number five was necessary because you can't have a secret club if somebody keeps telling her mom all the secrets. The "hiding bad papers" rule reflects a phase Kelsey went through where, if she got anything below an A on a school assignment, she hid the paper in her desk and wouldn't bring it home so we could see it, wrongly assuming she would get in trouble if we did. Evidently she didn't want other kids to get in trouble either. I think rules number seven and eight are essential for any club—kids or adults. You can't have burps or stink bombs going off when you're squeezed into close quarters! The rule about hitting is an obvious choice. The last rule, however, has always been my favorite: *Do your best.*

It's a basic human belief, even among seven-year-olds, that in order for relationships to work the people involved must be doing their best to make them work. This brings us to the second kind of distance we create when we're hurt—emotional distance.

Oddly enough, some of our deepest wounds come from people who haven't done anything severe enough for us to break off our relationship with them. They have given up caring, or they never learned how to express care in the first place. It's not that they've done anything bad enough to warrant, say, a divorce, but they haven't given everything they've got to grow and mature the relationship like we had hoped and expected. When we live with these kinds of relationships, we often wish the person we're connected to would do something severe so that we could distance ourselves geographically.

Norman Cousins wrote, "The tragedy of life is in what dies inside a man while he lives."[3] I think what dies inside people who guard their hearts and create emotional distance is the hope that their relationship will get better. They've resigned themselves to the fact that the person they're dealing with will always be the way he's always been.

I once bumped into a woman at the dry cleaner's whom Lisa and I met through my daughters' sports teams. She was one of those genuinely nice women who seem to have an enjoyable life: she was easygoing and pretty, she had nice kids and a very successful husband, and even though she had moved around a lot she seemed to have a lot of friends. Out of the blue she asked, "Do you think people can change?"

"Absolutely," I said. "I've seen people make dramatic changes."

"Then I want you to pray for my husband." She described how he had spent the last fifteen years of their marriage pursuing his corporate dream job at the expense of their relationship. "It's not that he's done anything immoral," she said. "I honestly wish he had. That would make it easier for me. It's just that there's nothing left inside of me that feels anything toward him. I've grown sick of waiting and tired of the apologies."

She's one of many women I've met over the years who have reminded me of Mary in Eugene O'Neill's play *Long Day's Journey into Night*, which is loosely based on the events of O'Neill's life. In the play, Mary's husband, James Tyrone, is a semisuccessful actor who has sacrificed time with Mary and their sons for the sake of his career, constantly moving them around in pursuit of the next applause.

The entire play focuses on just one day of their marriage, from eight-thirty in the morning until midnight. Scene by scene, hour by hour, the narrator peels back the layers of their tattered relationship until James is able to see the deep emotional damage he's caused his wife. Halfway through the play, as deeper conversations cause Mary to reveal her unfiltered feelings toward her husband, she callously confesses, "None of us can help the things life has done to us. They're done before you realize it, and once they're done they make you do other things until at last everything comes between you and what you'd like to be, and you've lost your true self forever."[4]

Emotionless in the face of Mary's unflinching despair, James wrestles with his responsibility for driving Mary to the edge. Finally, oblivious to what he has helped his wife become, James says to his sons, "The hardest thing to take is the blank wall she builds around her. Or it's more like a bank of fog in which she hides and loses herself. . . . You know something in her does it deliberately—to get beyond our reach, to be rid of us, to forget we're alive! It's as if, in spite of loving us, she hated us!"[5]

And from that point on, Mary turns inward and slowly begins to lose touch with reality; she's fearful, desperate, and alone.

Do "blank wall" and "bank of fog" describe the emotional distance you feel toward your husband, your wife, your father, your kids? I think Mary's right—sometimes things happen in life before we realize it, and those things really do come between who we are and what we'd like to become. Unlike Mary, however, I don't think it's a foregone conclusion that we lose our true selves forever. We could, but it's not inevitable—even if, like the woman I talked to outside the dry cleaner's, your marriage ends in divorce.

TOO MUCH DISTANCE

Herein lies the double-edged sword of creating geographical and emotional distance in our relationships. When we're hurt, creating distance is a good thing; distance guards our hearts. It allows us to heal and recover emotionally. It allows us to regain relational stability and plot our next course of action. Distance is a natural, healthy, God-honoring initial response to buy us time to figure out how to process what we're thinking and feeling. At the same time, forever keeping our distance is something we learn from spending too much time with the gorilla.

Gorillas are known for never sleeping in the same location twice. They are masters at creating space between themselves and those they fear. That's why the best gorilla researchers must first become great gorilla trackers. Temporarily creating distance is a good thing, but maintaining relational distance from people as a way of life is not. Trust me.

Keeping distance between ourselves and other people for too long reminds me of something that happened in my backyard just a few weeks ago. When I went outside to clean the barbecue grill to cook dinner on the back patio, I saw a robin fly out the hole on the side of the grill. Curious, I lifted the lid and discovered a nest with seven beautiful blue robin's eggs. Warning my kids not to touch the eggs, I allowed them to take pictures and gawk a few minutes before I closed the lid.

Several days later our family was elated when my youngest daughter, Camryn, was the first to hear the chirps of the chicks. I had never seen newborn birds before—so dependent and vulnerable. Not able to see yet, the seven newborns lifted their necks toward the sky, presumably hoping to be fed and to feel their mother's presence once again.

However, we were not prepared for what happened the next day. When we went out to see the hatchlings, we were greeted by a horrific sight: all seven birds lay dead in the nest, stretched over top of each other like a clump of night crawlers left in the sun too long. At first we thought the mother had abandoned them, but after thinking through all the possibilities, I concluded that the grill was to blame.

Unlike the uneven tree branches and bushes in our backyard, the grill offered the perfect accommodation for the robin's eggs. It was covered, which protected it from the elements, and its hard steel lid was impenetrable by outside intruders. Yet because the grill was black and had little room for air, the hot springtime sun that provided warmth for the eggs in the beginning became the very thing that ended up killing the chicks in the end.

The same thing happens when we remain distanced from people for too long. The place of safety inside ourselves that we retreat to eventually becomes the place where our lonely, relationally starved soul begins to die.

Every once in a while, I begin to develop a relationship with someone with whom I think I could become very close friends. Eventually I reach a point where a decision has to be made: will this friendship stay casual and above the surface, or will it move on to something much deeper and authentic? Almost every time I get to that point of decision, I feel the urge deep inside to push beyond the safety of the distance I've created—but then I quickly back away. For reasons that have absolutely nothing to do with this person, for reasons that have everything to do with the people I have failed to forgive, I feel myself pull back behind a bank of fog between us.

Every time I do this, I remind myself that I'm much happier living life this way. That's what I keep telling myself.

4

PESSIMISM

I appreciate the blessed fact of God's forgiveness, but I want something more than that: I want deliverance. I need forgiveness for what I have done, *but I need also deliverance from what I* am.

—Watchman Nee

2003 was not a good driving year for yours truly. I received three speeding tickets in nine months. My family will tell you it was four, but that last one didn't count because I went to the judge and groveled and got him to dismiss it, so technically there were only three. That third ticket, however, was a wake-up call.

We were driving late at night on the Pennsylvania Turnpike. I was going 62 miles per hour in a 55-miles-per-hour zone. (The police give you five extra miles per hour; I add two more!) When my daughters screamed, "Dad, you did it again!" I thought to myself, *You have got to be kidding me.* Sure enough, as I looked in the rearview mirror I saw the familiar lights, frown, and finger all working in tandem to point me to the side of the road. I knew the drill quite well, so as the officer walked to my window, I had my license and registration waiting.

"Sir, I clocked you going 73 miles per hour in a 55-miles-per-hour zone."

"No way," I shot back. "62 max. Maybe 65. Honest."

I thought being truthful about my speed would appeal to his sympathetic side. No such luck. The officer leaned forward and glanced inside the car at my wife and kids, while I sat there with my heart in my throat. After a few awkward seconds, he arched his back, pulled his ticket pad out, slid a pen out of his shirt pocket, and uttered the seven words no financially broke driver ever wants to hear: "Sir, give me your license and registration."

I couldn't believe it—three tickets in nine months! In twenty years of driving, I had received only one speeding ticket, and now this was my third in less than a year. Upset and not quite sure what to say next, I did something no thinking person in my position should ever do (unless you're the president or James Bond). I handed him my information and said glibly, "No problem officer. It just warms my heart to know that there's someone out tonight protecting the good citizens of Pennsylvania from treacherous criminals driving their kids to see their grandparents." His look and the $135 fine he handed me told me he didn't appreciate my humor.

Strangely, the rest of the drive I found myself thinking very little about the ticket and a great deal about how sarcastic I had become over the years—in my marriage, with my kids, among my friends, with everyone. With the Spirit's gentle conviction during the six uninterrupted hours I had while everyone else slept, I found myself slowly coming to the realization that my sarcasm was out of control.

Sarcasm is a strange habit. The word *sarcasm* originally comes from the Greek word that meant "to tear flesh."[1] When we are sarcastic, we cut others with our words. Sometimes it's done humorously; sometimes it's done caustically. However it's done, the ultimate result when we're sarcastic is that we slice people with our tongues.

Ephesians 4:29 tells us, "Do not let any unwholesome talk come out of your mouths, but only what is helpful for building others up according to their needs, that it may benefit those who listen." God is very clear: only use words that build people up. Keep tabs on your tongue. Do whatever it takes. Enter Sarcasm Anonymous; go into verbal recovery. Our relationships are at stake.

That drive to see my parents was during the holiday season. I thought it would be appropriate to make a New Year's resolution to spend the next year changing the way I communicated with people. I gave it my best shot. I prayed a lot. I memorized Scripture. I told people to pray for me. I kept a journal. I even read a book on the subject. I tried everything I knew to do to eliminate sarcasm from my speech. Yet nothing really seemed to help until, oddly enough, I stumbled upon an insight from the strangest of places—the ancient English poem *Beowulf*. [2]

Every day for twelve years, the monster Grendel rises up from his marshy home and breaks into nearby castles to eat the inhabitants. Eventually the heroic warrior Beowulf comes from a far-off land to rescue the terrorized country. A banquet is held in Beowulf's honor, but the celebration is cut short when Grendel bursts into the banquet hall and begins eating the king's warriors. Beowulf valiantly cuts off Grendel's right arm and sends the monster scurrying back home for good. Confident that his land is now secure, the king throws another banquet in the warrior Beowulf's honor.

The next night, however, something much more dreadful appears. Grendel's *mother* emerges from the marsh, takes back her son's right arm, and slithers away into the bog. Beowulf and the king's warriors rush to the edge of the water, and Beowulf dives in. Hundreds of feet below the surface, he eventually finds Grendel's mother hiding in her cave. A ferocious battle ensues, and Beowulf almost loses the fight. Then he discovers an ancient sword lying on the floor of the cave. He swiftly kills Grendel's mother and turns and decapitates Grendel himself.

Here's the lesson that helped me understand why I have had such a hard time getting rid of sarcasm: our problems never go away until we deal with what gave birth to them, the way Beowulf couldn't kill Grendel until he had first killed Grendel's mother. My biggest problem wasn't my sarcasm; my biggest problem was what gave birth to it. If I could deal with that, my sarcasm could begin to go away.

GOODNESS ECLIPSED

You want to know what I think is the saddest part about living with the gorilla? It's not that my heart has been jammed full of rage like an overstuffed suitcase. It's not that I've created this huge, stupid, impassable wall just outside the perimeter of my soul that continually separates me from those I want to get close to. Both of these realities have caused me tremendous amounts of pain, but I wouldn't say they've caused me great sadness. The most heartbreaking loss of all is the way the gorilla has slowly changed the way I view life itself. Living with the gorilla over time has altered the way I view people around me. My greatest problem isn't sarcasm, it's what gave birth to my sarcasm, and what gave birth to my sarcasm is the pessimistic way I view those I rub shoulders with on a daily basis—something I directly attribute to living with an unforgiving heart.

Genesis 1 in the Bible recounts the creation of the world. Like a cosmic Rembrandt, God spoke into existence life and beauty—a world teeming with possibility. After each day of creation, God stepped back with a smile as wide as the horizon and shouted throughout the expanse of the universe that what he had created was good! In fact, seven different times throughout the first chapter of Genesis, God looked at the world he created and said it was good:

> And God said, "Let there be light. . . . God saw that the light was good" (Genesis 1:3, 4).

> God called the dry ground "land," and the gathered waters he called "seas." And God saw that it was good (Genesis 1:10).

> The land produced vegetation. . . . And God saw that it was good (Genesis 1:12).

> God made two great lights. . . . And God saw that it was good (Genesis 1:16, 18).

> So God created the great creatures of the sea . . . and every winged bird. . . . And God saw that it was good (Genesis 1:21).

> God made the wild animals according to their kinds. . . . And God saw that it was good (Genesis 1:25).

So God created man in his own image. . . . God saw all
that he had made, and it was very good (Genesis 1:27, 31).

To me, the saddest thing about living with the gorilla is that he's convinced me not to buy into God's perspective on the world anymore. I struggle with seeing most people as inherently good. Don't get me wrong: I believe what the Bible teaches; we are all broken people. But part of working with God to redeem the world means treating people the way we were initially created, the way we want them to become, not the way they actually are now. And that's where my greatest struggle lies.

I desperately want to view people the way God says they can become, but something began to die the day I was humiliated in the courtroom, as I described in chapter 1. It was the beautiful, innocent, childlike way I viewed people and the world. As if someone flipped a switch inside me, my genuine, natural exuberance was replaced with bitter pessimism. That trial, coupled with incredibly painful events that have happened since then, situations that I'm still processing and can't find the strength to write about yet—words too harsh, intentions so cruel, needless, careless, dark—these things forever altered the way I view people and the world.

Pessimism is the tendency to expect the worst possible outcome in any circumstance. Deep down, whether we want to admit it or not, one of the reasons we struggle with forgiveness is that we're pessimists. Don't you long for the days when you didn't constantly analyze people's faults and you saw everyone with purer motives? Don't you long for the days when you thought the next day and the one after that would only be better than today? Esperanza, the main character in Sandra

Cisneros's novel *The House on Mango Street*, describes her grandmother as someone who "looked out the window her whole life, the way so many women sit their sadness on an elbow."[3] I wonder what she was struggling to see. Was it goodness in the people around her? I wonder what sent her to that window ledge.

I wonder what kind of weight you're placing on your elbow right now.

A NATURAL RESPONSE

My first day in seminary, a guy who looked like he'd just moved to Princeton from a commune sat down next to me in the cafeteria. He was wearing the prototypical tie-dyed T-shirt, Birkenstock sandals, long scruffy beard, and a necklace full of beads and arrowheads. After introducing himself and making small talk, he began peppering me with theological questions. I think he could tell I was one of the token evangelical students on campus and somehow felt inclined to liberate me from a narrow-minded view of Christianity. After asking what I thought happens to people of other religions when they die, he cut me off before I could answer.

"Dude," he said. "Like, here's the deal, man. Me and a friend of mine, we were at a Grateful Dead concert and, like, tripping on acid. In the middle of the concert, something happened that totally freaked me out, man. My friend was tripping and had this vision where God appeared to him as a man, with a moustache, blue jeans, and cowboy boots. He told me about it and I was like, 'Whoa, dude, no way.' I told him that I had a vision of God too, except in my vision God appeared as a woman with long blond hair, a voluptuous figure, and wearing high heels. When I told him that, we just kind of stood there and freaked out because we both knew that God was trying to tell us it didn't matter what religion we belonged to, as long as we believed in God. Dude, that concert changed my life."

After a long, awkward pause, I got up and said, "Well, all righty then, dude, I'll be seeing you later!"

I never talked to him again. I literally never had a conversation with him again. Not because of the way he dressed, or his nutty theology, or the way he challenged my belief system. I avoided him because of his aggression toward me, the way he seemed to single me out and pursue me. He may have been the greatest guy in the world, or the creepiest. All I know is that I wasn't interested in finding out, simply because I didn't trust him. It's hard to trust people again after you've been hurt.

I think it's important to recognize that pessimism is simply a natural result of getting our souls trampled on by somebody with skin on them. We didn't get this way because we have deficient character or missed some important aspect of moral development in our early childhood years. Pessimism, for most people, is something that arrives on the coattails of pain. Mistrust is a learned response. The reason we have trouble trusting people is that people have broken our trust. If we had never been hurt by anyone, we would not have a problem with trust; it's that simple. This reminds me of something psychologists call classical conditioning.

Researchers have learned that hungry dogs, placed in a cage with a pedal attached to a food dispenser, will learn to press the pedal to get food. The dog has a cushy set-up until the clinician attaches an electric wire to the pedal so that a shock is administered along with the food. The dog will initially pull away from the pedal, but over time forgets the pain associated with pushing the pedal and tries to secure food again. Eventually, however, after getting repeatedly zapped, the dog is conditioned to associate the pedal with the pain of the electric shock, and it stops trying to secure food altogether.

The same thing has happened to you and me, but instead of reaching out to push a pedal for food, we reached out to those around us for love and connection. Instead of finding what we expected, we were lied to, or dumped for someone younger, or forced to choose in a divorce court which parent we would spend the rest of our childhood with. When that happened, something inside us said that we'd better start looking for the worst in people instead of the best.

WEARY FOR CHANGE

This is why I think obeying Jesus' command in Matthew 7:1 is almost impossible until we get rid of the gorilla. "Do not judge, or you too will be judged." Was Jesus serious? Making judgments about people and their motives is what allows us to predict who will hurt us and who is safe. I think this is why sarcasm is so hard for me to shake. Sarcasm is nothing more than my humorous way to keep people at arm's length until I know I can trust them enough to let them come closer. The whole time I'm doing it, I'm judging them, evaluating their posture, sizing up their game plan, learning more and more about whether they have my best interest in mind.

Wouldn't you agree, however, that this constant sizing up of people gets old? Thomas Merton warned, "You are made in the image of what you desire."[4] I've grown weary of what I've become; the way

I look into the eyes of people I don't know, the way I constantly second guess people's motives. I want to stop myself before I'm completely reshaped into something ugly and defensive and it's too late to change. I want some part of my childlike innocence back. I want to know what it's like to genuinely trust people again.

I think that's what was happening in the story of Jesus and the woman caught in adultery in John 8. As the crowd stood around the woman, clutching their stones in both hands, Jesus looked into their eyes and said, "If any one of you is without sin, let him be the first one to throw a stone at her" (John 8:7). John records something that I have always only glanced at until recently: "At this, those who heard began to go away one at a time, the older ones first" (v. 9).

Why the older ones first? What was it about the older people in the crowd that made them walk away first? Maybe it was that they were older and wiser. Maybe they were the most ashamed. Honestly, no one will ever really know for sure. John doesn't tell us.

My best guess: they were tired of judging. They wanted to experience how good it felt to trust again, while they still had time.

GORILLA DNA

5

MYTHS

Forgiveness—true forgiveness—takes time. It is a process you must not short-circuit. When you forgive too quickly, without adequately working through what has happened and how you feel about it, your forgiveness is incomplete.

—DR. DAVID STOOP

Drinking beer will send you to hell. And not just to hell, but to the hottest part of hell, the place where atheists, mass murderers, and Yankee fans go when they die. At least that's what I was told when I was growing up.

To be fair, no one ever actually showed me a passage in the Bible that condemned the consumption of alcohol. I just assumed it had to be in there because, growing up, I never met a Christian who drank. Not one. My mom and dad didn't. None of my Sunday school teachers touched the stuff, and certainly not my pastor. At least none of them drank in front of me.

In fact, until I was sixteen the only person I ever witnessed regularly drinking alcohol was my grandfather. But even then, I didn't know it was alcohol. My grandmother told me that the strange concoction

Grandpa had with his dinner every evening was "Grandpa's medicine." Evidently drinking will send you to hell, but lying will not.

You can understand, then, my utter shock when my wife said I should occasionally be seen with a beer in my hand to help me build more effective friendships with men in our community who weren't churchgoers.

"Ain't doing it."

"Why?"

"Besides going to hell?"

"That's ridiculous. Just hold it in your hand. It will put guys at ease and let them know you don't judge them. Then when they have their guard down, you can have a spiritual conversation."

Lisa had a point. Where we live, drinking beer with a meal is like having a soft drink; there's no moral baggage to it. Especially at social gatherings, it's expected and somewhat assumed. And I'm pretty sure the Bible teaches that getting hammered is the real issue, not having a beer.

"OK, I'll test your theory," I said. "The next time I'm with a group of guys and they ask me if I want a beer, I'm grabbing one."

Four months later, my daughter's soccer team had a backyard barbeque to celebrate the end of their season. None of the parents were Christians, although one guy had visited my church the previous Sunday.

Halfway through the party, Frank, our host, yelled out, "The Phillies are in the middle of the seventh inning, if anyone wants to watch the game in the house!" Suddenly all the men dropped what they were doing and stampeded toward the door.

"Beer, anyone?" Frank asked as we got settled in his family room.

This is it, I thought. *This is my chance to find out if having a beer will make guys feel more comfortable talking to me when I bring up spiritual matters.*

"Pass me one of those bad boys," I said in a deep voice. I took a huge gulp. "Aaaaah. That's what I'm talking about." Silently I prayed, *This better work.*

"Who else wants one?" Frank asked, standing in front of the television with two bottles in each hand. "Bill, how 'bout you? Want a beer? I've got plenty!"

"No, it's a school night."

Huh?

"How about you, Ted? Want to knock back a few tonight?"

"Honestly, Frank, my daughter and I have been having these talks about alcohol, and I've decided to stop drinking. You know, the whole trying-to-be-an-example kind of thing."

"Jim, surely you want one, don't you?"

"I'm with Ted. I never touch the stuff."

I panicked. I wanted to die. I sank back into my chair and tried to disappear. I couldn't believe it. None of the guys took a sip of alcohol. Not one. And there I was, chugging beer like a college kid at a frat party, while the men I wanted to influence began discussing the moral quandaries of drinking.

OK, I thought, *calm down. These guys don't know what I do for a living. I'll just s-l-o-w-l-y tuck the bottle under my chair and act like nothing happened.* But before I could do that, the guy who visited my church the previous weekend sat down on the couch next to me, patted my shoulder, and said loud enough for everyone to hear, "Awesome sermon Sunday!"

I looked down at the Budweiser in my hand and thought, *I'm going to kill my wife.*

Later that evening, when I walked through our kitchen door, my wife smiled and asked, "How did the party go?"

I stopped midstride, lifted one eyebrow, and said, "It was a virtual Billy Graham crusade. Thanks for asking."

DEBUNKING THE MYTHS

Now, you would think that later that night my wife and I had a good laugh about this, kissed, rolled over, and went to sleep. That all happened, except the rolling over and falling right to sleep part. Instead, I began to replay in my mind how embarrassed I felt at Frank's house. I knew it was a trivial incident, embarrassingly trivial, but that didn't seem to matter. The more I thought about how awkward and embarrassed I felt that evening, the more perturbed I became. I didn't know who I was upset at exactly—me, Lisa, or both of us—but I was upset.

Then it happened again: when I got up the next morning, there stood the gorilla. He stared at me, nudging me with his paws to say something mean to Lisa and start the day off on the wrong foot. Eventually, thank goodness, basic adult maturity prevailed. I got up, looked at myself in the mirror, and thought, *Quit taking yourself so seriously, Brian. Have a good laugh and drop it.* And I did. I shrugged my shoulders and had a good chuckle; then I got in the shower and didn't think about it anymore.

We've all experienced minor irritations like that, but unfortunately we've also experienced situations that we couldn't shrug off quite that easily. Many of those events were painful. Some were unbearable, some even ghastly. It's impossible for me to know what your journey has been, but one thing I know for certain: once word got out that you struggle with an unforgiving heart, well-meaning Christians began offering you really dumb advice.

I don't know why, but when some Christians discover that their friends are struggling with the gorilla, they begin wildly quoting Bible verses like a gunslinger in a Wild West shoot-out. As you can probably attest, having friends pull a spiritual Wyatt Earp doesn't make things better, for at least two very good reasons. First, no one likes to hear advice from someone who hasn't been where we've been, even if it is coming from God's Word. Second, the Bible verses that get slung around about forgiveness are typically misinterpreted.

Missing the mark on what a Bible passage means wouldn't be so bad if the issue at hand were gardening or fishing or whether God has a favorite NASCAR driver. But we're dealing with forgiveness; we ought to be 100 percent dead-on accurate with how we apply what the Bible says. Those of us who have been living with the gorilla have nasty scars and relational wounds that make us willing to consider taking or buying or doing *anything* to stop the pain. Getting the wrong understanding of what the Bible teaches is spiritually lethal—it leaves us with guilt-ridden faith and distorted views of God, and both tempt us to throw Christianity out altogether.

What I want to do in the rest of this chapter is debunk what I consider the two most common forgiveness myths Christians toss around. My hunch is that if you've been wrestling with an unforgiving heart, you've heard these already. I think it's essential to discard the myths before we can start talking about real solutions.

MYTH #1: FORGIVENESS EQUALS RECONCILIATION

The first myth that needs to be addressed is the belief that in order to genuinely forgive someone I must be willing to meet with him or her and try to bring about some measure of reconciliation between the two of us.

When my oldest daughter entered first grade, my wife and I anxiously attended Mrs. White's first grade back-to-school night to hear her philosophy of classroom management and her expectations for the students. Partway through her lecture, Mrs. White directed our attention to two small chairs facing each other at the side of the classroom. On the back of each seat hung a sign that read Talk About It Chairs.

"I believe children need to learn early on how to resolve their differences," Mrs. White said. "So whenever a conflict arises, it's my practice to send the children involved to the Talk About It Chairs to work through their problem. Once they are finished, they can leave and go back to their classroom duties."

"What if they can't work it out?" I asked.

"They stay there until they do," Mrs. White replied.

Then another parent joked, "We're the ones who need those chairs."

I think if we adults are being honest, we know that we could have Talk About It Chairs in every room of our lives and we'd still choose to live with the gorilla.

The reasons are obvious: We've tried the Talk About It Chairs and we don't like them. Or we're afraid we won't. They're uncomfortable—too hard, and they hurt our backs. The process takes too long. Living with the gorilla is the path of least resistance. It's part of our human nature; we do what we think will cause us the least amount of pain. If it were easier to express anger appropriately and genuinely listen to others, accepting responsibility for our actions and pain as part of the human journey, we would choose the Talk About It Chairs. But it's not, so we choose living with the gorilla.

For most people, finally going to the Talk About It Chairs with the person who hurt us will be a key part of the process of getting rid of the gorilla. But what if that person is unwilling to go there with us? What if going to the chairs would cause a tremendous amount of unwarranted pain for me and my loved ones? What if attempts at reconciliation would end up causing more harm than good? God's answer is simple: don't attempt reconciliation.

Forgiveness and reconciliation are two similar but unrelated actions. You *can* have one without the other. Forgiveness is something you can do on your own; reconciliation takes two parties. Forgiveness is unilateral; reconciliation can't happen if two people won't sit down at the chairs. Forgiveness is commanded in Scripture (Colossians 3:13, 14). Reconciliation is not commanded but is highly suggested *if possible* (Romans 12:18).

Jesus taught in Matthew 7:6: "Do not give dogs what is sacred; do not throw your pearls to pigs. If you do, they may trample them under their feet, and then turn and tear you to pieces." No one really knows for certain what Jesus was referring to when he used the word *sacred*. Many think he meant the message of the Christian faith. Others think it was faith in general. I think what Jesus meant by the word *sacred* is our hearts. God is realistic. Sometimes it just isn't possible to reconcile without getting our hearts trampled on and ripped to pieces. Because our hearts are sacred and vulnerable, sometimes reconciliation is not in our best interest. Sometimes it's not spiritually healthy for the other person either.

Maybe the person who hurt you has passed away, and you can't reconcile even if you want to. Maybe you need to evaluate the benefit of reconciliation and possibly attempt to reconcile. Regardless of what Christians may have told you in the past, your ability to forgive is not dependent on a storybook ending with hugs, warm fuzzies, and waves good-bye as you drive away into the sunset with a tear running down your cheek. You can still get rid of the gorilla without having the person who hurt you meet you at the Talk About It Chairs.

MYTH #2: IF I DON'T FORGIVE, GOD WON'T FORGIVE ME

I'll never forget a compelling sermon I heard years ago on the topic of forgiveness. The basis for the message that day was Matthew 6:14, 15: "For if you forgive men when they sin against you, your heavenly Father will also forgive you. But if you do not forgive men their sins, your Father will not forgive your sins."

The pastor talked at length about the fact that God loves us so much he is willing to use the threat of hell to force us to wake up and forgive those who hurt us. With passion in his voice, he talked about how awful it would be not to go to heaven for all eternity because of some temporary though painful event that happened to us on earth. Pacing back and forth across the stage, he told story after emotional story to try to convince his listeners to let go of the past and move on. Then, with tears in his eyes, he concluded his message with a heart-felt plea to forgive those who hurt us while we still had time.

After the service, I walked to my car and thought to myself, *That guy's an idiot.* I was shocked, for two reasons: I couldn't believe such a negative thing would come to mind so shortly after a church service; I expected more restraint. More important, I was the guy who preached that sermon. The whole time I was speaking, I was thinking to myself, *Wait a minute, this doesn't sound right, even if it is exactly what these verses seem to be saying. There's got to be more to the story.*

I was confused. I had been repeating exactly what I heard my pastor teach while I was growing up and exactly what my seminary professors had taught me in their classes. In fact, the more I thought about it, the more I realized that I had never heard any other interpretation of Matthew 6:14, 15 anywhere—not in the churches I'd attended, not on the radio or on television, not from Christian friends—not anywhere.

I was disturbed. My questioning seemed heresy filled. I began studying what great Christian leaders throughout church history thought about this passage. I was shocked to discover that they taught the same things I had preached! Look at what some of the most influential pastors and theologians in two thousand years of church history said about the need to forgive in order to be forgiven:

> The man who does not from his heart forgive him who repents of his sin, and asks forgiveness, need not suppose that his own sins are forgiven of God.—St. Augustine[1]

> God has promised us assurance that everything is forgiven and pardoned, yet on the condition that we also forgive our neighbor. . . . If you do not forgive, do not think that God forgives you.—Martin Luther[2]

The only Law of admission to His forgiveness is that we pardon our brothers for any sin against us.—John Calvin[3]

A forgiving spirit . . . is a sign that we are in a state of forgiveness and favour ourselves: and that, if we are not of such a spirit, we are not forgiven of God.—Jonathan Edwards[4]

I realize that it's pretty audacious of me to disagree with some of the greatest theologians of all time, but I have to humbly and graciously break rank with them: *Our forgiveness is not dependent upon our forgiving others.* Let me explain why.

JUDGMENT IS AN OLD COVENANT CONSEQUENCE

When Jesus taught that to be forgiven one must forgive, who was he talking to?

The Bible shows us God relating to people in two different ways at two different times. The first way is called the Old Covenant. If the people of ancient Israel obeyed God's commands, they received God's blessing and favor. If they disobeyed God's commands, they didn't. That's really oversimplifying it, but basically that's how it worked.

When God sent his Son Jesus to die on the cross, that event initiated a new way for God to relate to us. No longer is the status of our relationship with God based on commands we obey, but upon God's grace and mercy. This new arrangement is called the New Covenant, and it is the way God relates to us now.

Jesus lived under and taught from the perspective of the Old Covenant. Those who listened to him lived under the Old Covenant as well. All the Israelites from the time of Moses until Jesus' death and resurrection lived under the arrangement of the Old Covenant and had to obey God's commands to receive his blessings. Most people assume, because the four Gospels (Matthew, Mark, Luke, and John) are found in the New Testament section of the Bible, that Jesus' teachings contained in the gospels were taught from the perspective of the New Covenant. That's not the case.

When Jesus said that in order to be forgiven one must forgive others, that's exactly what that teaching meant *to the people who lived under the Old Covenant arrangement.* Their relationship with God was based on their obedience to the law. How did Jesus respond when the rich young ruler approached him and asked, "What must I do to inherit eternal life?" (Mark 10:17). "You know the commands," he said (v. 19), reminding the young man which Old Covenant commands he needed to obey to go to heaven. Jesus replied as any person living under the Old Covenant would have. I believe that the situation was the same for those who first heard Jesus' teaching about forgiveness—their relationship with God depended upon obedience to the commands of the Old Covenant.

OUR RELATIONSHIP WITH GOD IS BASED ON GRACE, NOT WORKS

For years I squirmed whenever I read or heard Matthew 25:41-43: "Then he will say to those on his left, 'Depart from me, you who are cursed, into the eternal fire prepared for the devil and his angels.

For I was hungry and you gave me nothing to eat, I was thirsty and you gave me nothing to drink, I was a stranger and you did not invite me in, I needed clothes and you did not clothe me, I was sick and in prison and you did not look after me.'" I thought, *I'd better get out there and start visiting prisoners or inviting hitchhikers to spend the night, or God won't let me into heaven.* I was always consumed with fear, thinking that there might be something I wasn't doing that would keep me out of heaven. I didn't fully understand how my relationship with God works under the New Covenant. Ephesians 2:8, 9 spells it out: "For it is by grace you have been saved, through faith—and this not from yourselves, it is the gift of God—not by works, so that no one can boast."

We can be confident in the status of our relationship with God because God's continual acceptance of us is not based on our obedience to the Old Covenant law but upon our response to God's grace. With this in mind, what we have to do is go back to passages like the one in Matthew 25 and reinterpret them from our perspective as people living within the New Covenant of grace. Feeding the poor and caring for prisoners are incredibly important activities for Christians, but we do them now because of our love for God and his love for hurting people, not because we're afraid God will send us to hell.

It's the same way with Jesus' teaching on forgiveness. The reason we forgive people now, under the New Covenant, is because of our desire to please God and because forgiving those who hurt us is the best way to live, not because we're afraid we'll go to hell if we don't. Simply put, even though we'll be miserable if we choose to live with the gorilla rather than forgive, we can still confidently know that we're going to heaven. Why? Because our standing with God is not altered by our obedience to certain commands, including the one about forgiveness.

If you get only one thing out of this chapter, I hope it's this: authentic forgiveness never occurs when we feel coerced to forgive. Unless you want it to happen and are willing to do the hard work to make it happen, forgiveness will never take place. Forgiveness takes time. It is a process. Sometimes it takes a long while to drop our rocks.

There's a wonderful book in print that has an equally bad title. *The Art of Forgiveness*. Genuine forgiveness is anything but an art. To me the process of forgiving resembles the front line of a battlefield— confusion, lots of screaming, and very little indication whether we're making progress until much later. Forgiveness is a lengthy, miraculous, convoluted process that takes place because people want it to happen, not because they're backed into it.

Years ago as a pastor fresh out of seminary, I sat down with a man who had been sexually abused as a child. We talked at length about how he felt like a prisoner trapped inside his memories and how much he wanted to find the strength to forgive. Part way into our conversation, he said that he just wasn't ready to forgive yet, so I opened my Bible, turned to the passage we've been discussing, and read it to him as lovingly as I could. Then I recited the traditional interpretation of what those verses mean and how that applied to his situation.

I'll never forget his blank stare and what he said next: "I don't know much about the Bible, but it's pretty clear that the person who wrote that had no idea what it's like to be raped by his grandfather."

Then he walked out, and I never saw him again.

6

BELIAL

There are two equal and opposite errors into which our race can fall about the devils. One is to disbelieve in their existence. The other is to believe, and to feel an excessive and unhealthy interest in them.

—C. S. Lewis

So far we've discussed how an unforgiving heart begins when pain chooses us. When we're unable to release that pain, the gorilla amasses size and strength and over time instigates three specific changes in our lives:

- We move from expressing anger over a painful incident to allowing our hearts to become consumed with rage.
- We create distance in our relationships as we try to protect ourselves from future pain.
- We become overly pessimistic about the nature and motives of other people.

In addition, our attempts to find the strength to forgive are frustrated by the myths about forgiveness we have learned in the past. And there's another unseen force aimed against us too. I didn't understand its impact until something happened to me years ago that forever defined the way I look at the gorilla.

A FRIGHTENING ENCOUNTER

What I remember most about first meeting Kathy were her expensive, perfectly pressed business suits; they exuded personal mastery. As I would soon find out, however, the suits were an odd contrast to what was really going on inside Kathy's soul. At fifty-six, Kathy was at the peak of her professional corporate career, but internally she had grown weary of keeping one step ahead of her past. I was fresh out of seminary when God brought Kathy to the church I served, and I had never seriously counseled anyone, let alone someone who carried as much pain as she.

Kathy approached me after church one day and asked if we could set up an appointment to talk.

"Sure," I said. "What about?"

"Stuff."

"Can you give me an idea of what's on your mind?"

"Weird stuff going on in my life."

Must be having marital issues, I thought. "OK, I'm free at one on Tuesday. Does that work? I'll see you at the church office."

She was at my office door at 12:55 sharp.

"So how can I help?"

"Let's just say I've got problems."

I leaned forward, waiting to hear what she would say next.

"I'm here as a last resort. My counselor got rid of me. She told me to go find a pastor because she had tried everything she knew to do."

"You're kidding, right? What could be so bad that a therapist would fire a client?"

Suddenly Kathy's expression changed, and she stared directly into my eyes and said in a monotone voice, "If you can't help me, I'm going to kill myself."

Oh, no. I'm in way over my head. "Listen, Kathy," I fired back, "you're not going to kill yourself. Not today. Not tomorrow. Not ever. Not on my watch. There's no problem you'll ever face that is so big that God can't help you deal with it, so why don't you just share what's going on so we can work toward a solution? Did someone do something to you? Are you in trouble with the law? What is it?"

After a long pause, she took a deep breath and shared what still haunts me to this day. "They did things."

I sat there, silent, not knowing quite how to respond. After a few awkward moments, I asked, "What things?"

"Ceremonies."

"I don't understand. What kind of ceremonies?"

"They did horrible things to me. They made me do horrible things too." She began sobbing uncontrollably, unable to get more than a few sentences out without having to stop to catch her breath.

I moved my chair around the table and put my hand on her shoulder. Her speech, the penetrating look of her eyes, the way her shoulders shook as she recalled each horrifying detail from her past—it all reminded me of that line in Hamlet:

"And in this harsh world draw thy breath in pain,
To tell my story."[1]

Over an hour later, I had finally pieced together the grisly details of Kathy's past. Her family—parents, grandparents, aunts, uncles— was deeply involved in the occult when she was growing up; they kidnapped hitchhikers and brought them back to the family farm and murdered them in satanic rituals in the barn.

The victims, Kathy said, were drugged and laid on a makeshift altar with their hands and feet tied together. Before the murders, Kathy was repeatedly raped and beaten by the older members of the family, to the point of nearly losing control of her faculties. The first time this took place, the family was afraid Kathy would tell the police or her teachers, so they took the dead body, threw it in a casket, and then put Kathy inside the casket too and nailed it shut and left her there all night. In the morning, they told her that if she ever told anyone, they would put her inside another corpse-filled casket and leave her there for good.

They did worse things, if you can imagine things more unspeakable than these. Slowly drawing her breath in pain, Kathy shared stories about strange symbols, chanting, ghastly rituals, and how eerie it was when things went back to normal when all of this was done—in particular, how her grandmother would clean up after the ceremonies ended, go into the kitchen, and cook everyone dinner as if nothing had ever happened.

"How old were you when this first started?" I asked.

"Seven."

I felt sick to my stomach and didn't know what to say. As Kathy talked, I just kept repeating, "I am so sorry this happened to you. I am so sorry. I am so sorry."

Then she said, "The reason I'm here is it's been almost fifty years, and I still can't escape the memories. I hate my family. They're all dead, every single one of them, but I can still hear their voices in my head. I can still smell the stench of those bodies on top of me. Brian, I still smell their stench in my dreams. I hate my family for what they did to me. I'll never get past this until I forgive them. Can you please help me so I can move on with my life?"

When I heard the word *forgive*, I felt like I finally had something to offer. I grabbed Kathy's hand and told her that although I had never experienced anything like what she had gone through, I did know a little bit about the struggle to forgive. I told her my story and explained that I was willing to help her if she really wanted me to do so. "The first step is to make sure you have your relationship with God squared away. You need to know how much you matter to God and what his Son Jesus did for you on the cross."

"I did that. I became a Christian one year ago this month. It was beautiful."

I reached back to my bookshelf. "OK, then the next step is to read this book on forgiveness. It's written by a wonderful Christian psychologist. He's really going to be able to help you put into perspective why you've had such a struggle after all these years and what you can do about it. Read this and then we'll get together again in a few weeks."

"I already read it. It doesn't help."

"What do you mean, it doesn't help?"

"Things float."

"Things float?"

"Yeah, things float. I'll wake up in the middle of the night and shoes will be floating across the room. That guy doesn't talk about spirits making stuff float in his book. I'll wake up, see red eyes in the mirror staring back at me, and stuff will be floating across the room."

"Floating shoes, huh?" I had been duped. *Red eyes? Nike low-top running shoes flying out of the closest? Come on.*

"Seriously," she said. "I'm not making this stuff up. You don't believe me, do you?"

"I believe that you believe that you see these things."

I can't believe I've wasted an entire afternoon with this lady.

"I tell you what, I have a meeting that I'm late for, so why don't we pray, you reread that book, and then get back in touch with me when you're done and we'll talk." *Floating shoes.*

After we prayed, I escorted her to the door. As she walked away, she turned back and said, "I have to warn you. They might come after you. That's really why my other therapist quit on me. Things happened to her and she flipped out."

Lady, I thought, *the only people who will be coming are the nice people in white coats to take you to the nuthouse.* "Thanks for the head's up."

Flashing Lights and Bad Tuna

A little later I called it a day and left for home. Half a mile from my house, my car's engine started making noises and shaking violently. Since I wasn't too far from home, I decided to keep driving. Moments later, I pulled into my driveway, right as the engine died.

I can't believe this! I thought. *I just got this stupid car fixed!*

When I pushed the garage door opener, the door didn't budge. I tried it again. Nothing. Again. Nothing. "Brilliant!" I shouted, throwing my arms in the air. "My day just couldn't get any better!"

When I walked into the kitchen, I found a note from Lisa telling me that she and the girls had gone shopping and leftovers were in the fridge. *Great, leftovers!* I prepared a plate, placed it in the microwave, and pressed start. Five seconds later the kitchen lights flashed off and on and a puff of smoke came out the back of the microwave. I hit the start button again—nothing. I checked the breaker box— no flipped switches—and as I closed the breaker box door, the words "They might come after you" popped into my head.

"That's nonsense," I said out loud. "It's all a coincidence."

No sooner did those words come out of my mouth than my stomach started twitching and grumbling. *Huh, I think I'm coming down with a bug.* Two hours later I was hovering over the toilet, puking my guts out.

"God, I think I need your help here," I prayed as I lay on the bathroom floor.

To say that I was more than a little freaked out is an understatement. If this was some kind of spiritual attack—and by that time I was convinced that it was—then God had sent the wrong guy to fight the battle. I'm a chicken. My wife and kids joke with me all the time that they think I have that "startling disease" you see on the news every once in a while—for no reason I'll jump back and gasp loudly, startling myself and everyone around me. It's worse around Halloween.

Once I went on a very tame "haunted hayride" with my children when all three of them were much younger. The wagon was meandering through a tranquil rolling farm, when suddenly two people wearing masks came out of a cornfield. It was an age-appropriate event, designed to let preschoolers have a little bit of fun, but that didn't matter to me.

As soon as I saw them heading for the wagon, I let out a high-pitched scream, grabbed my youngest daughter, and lunged overtop my two older ones into the center of the wagon. Hay went flying. Babies started crying. It was quite a scene. As I slowly turned around, all the other parents in the wagon began pulling their children closer to them. Thoroughly embarrassed, Lisa just sat there shaking her head.

"What?" I said. "That clown was scary!"

FLAMING ARROWS AND THE SHIELD OF FAITH

When Lisa came home with the girls, I was already in bed, lights out, trying to fall asleep as a way to find some relief from the nausea. Later I developed quite a nasty fever and floated in and out of sleep. Sometime in the middle of the night, something mystical and strange happened. I had a brief dream about an old man placing a ram's skull on top of his head. In my dream I must have somehow startled him because when he turned around, he began running toward me, which in turn completely terrified me. When the old man saw my fearful reaction, his entire mouth opened up, wide and fiendish, mythical like a dragon's mouth, full of sharp teeth and fire. I fell backward in fear. As he lunged toward me, just inches from my face, suddenly a shield appeared, separating us and saving my life. On the shield was written "Ephesians 6:16."

I woke up drenched in sweat. My heart was pounding. Wondering what that Scripture meant, I pushed the covers back, grabbed the Bible off my nightstand, went to the family room and turned on the light. *This kind of stuff only happens to my Pentecostal friends,*

I thought. I found Ephesians and ran my finger down chapter six until my eyes landed on verse 16: "Take up the shield of faith, with which you can extinguish all the flaming arrows of the evil one."

Trembling, I took that verse as a message from God. I got down on my knees, confessed to God that I was scared out of my mind, and cried out for help. I told him that this whole thing was way bigger and more complex than I would ever understand. I told him I had absolutely no idea what I was doing. I told him I was ashamed for the glib way I had treated Kathy at the end of our meeting, and I apologized for trying to help her in my own strength. I apologized for thinking that I could lead people to forgiveness based on human insight and experience alone. I told God that Kathy's problem was much larger, much deeper, and much more serious than I was able to handle myself. When I finished, I just lay there, facedown, trembling, humbled.

Needless to say, I didn't wait for Kathy to contact me. The next morning I called her and begged her to meet me at the office as soon as she could possibly be there. I told her what happened the night before and apologized for my arrogance. Then I asked for the book back that I had given her. "What we're dealing with isn't going to be fazed by the latest pop-psychology book with a few Bible verses sprinkled in. Kathy, if you really want to find a path to forgiveness, we're going to have to take up the shield of faith."

LOOKING BEYOND OUR WORLD

That experience forever changed the way I view the problem of an unforgiving heart. Why? Up until I met Kathy, I had always thought of forgiveness as a transaction between two people—an entirely human process from beginning to end:

One human hurts another, and that human reels from the pain.

Other humans gather around the hurt human, sharing their collective human wisdom and experience on how they've recovered from prior injuries themselves.

If the hurt human can't find a way to forgive, a professional human is called in to help. This human-fixing specialist—educated, trained, and licensed by other humans—guides the hurt human to freedom.

Over time, strengthened by the support and insights of the collective human condition, the wounded human being hopefully finds the support to forgive and can move on.

Here's the problem: What if the reason we humans have trouble getting rid of the gorilla is that there are larger, darker, more powerful forces at work with a vested interest in keeping us from forgiving the person who hurt us? And what if the key to finding a path to forgiveness lies not so much upon heeding the counsel of other humans around us, but on leaning upon the only one who can truly overcome the forces of darkness both inside and outside our world?

Here are two things you must understand if you want to get rid of the gorilla.

SATAN WANTS TO KEEP YOU TRAPPED

There's a lot about that experience with Kathy that I'm still unsure of even after all these years. I'm unsure about the red eyes in the mirror. I myself find it hard to believe, but I'm not saying Kathy was lying. Floating shoes? A few people I know have told me they've experienced similar things, but then again, they probably think Elvis is still alive too. That night—the car, the garage door, the microwave, getting sick—it all could have been a coincidence. The car was old. The house was old. The microwave was a very old wedding gift. I might have eaten a really bad tuna melt earlier in the day, and I know I've had stranger dreams.

One thing I do know to be true: Satan is real, and he was not about to let Kathy forgive those who hurt her in the past without a fight. His presence was tangible over the months that followed that initial meeting. In fact, we almost lost Kathy, multiple times. Her struggle was long, intense, dark, and debilitating for everyone involved. Eventually, through the tireless support of a small group of people in our church and the help of a godly Christian psychiatrist, Kathy got her feet firmly planted on the path to forgiveness and wholeness.

Through the years I've often wondered why Satan's grasp was so tight on her. Studying the Lord's Prayer in Matthew 6 has helped me answer this question.

The Lord's Prayer contains two of the most studied and discussed statements about forgiveness that Jesus ever uttered:

> Forgive us our debts, as we also have forgiven our debtors (Matthew 6:12).

> For if you forgive men when they sin against you, your heavenly Father will also forgive you. But if you do not forgive men their sins, your Father will not forgive your sins (Matthew 6:14, 15).

These verses serve as the basis for just about everything we know that Jesus taught about forgiveness. The "Forgive us our debts" statement is right in the body of the Lord's Prayer itself, while the other verses come at the end, like a bookend, underscoring the need to forgive others while we are praying.

I once was meditating on the Lord's Prayer when an insight jumped out at me. In between these famous verses on forgiveness is another statement by Jesus. I always glossed right over it, focusing on the verses about forgiveness instead and not realizing the significance of where this statement is placed. But the more I read and reread the entire prayer in context, the more I realized there was something I had been missing all along. Matthew 6:13 says, "And lead us not into temptation, but deliver us from the evil one."

Notice two things: First, Jesus said that we should pray for deliverance, not from evil in general, but from the evil *one*, referring to Satan. Jesus believed in the literal reality of Satan as a force that could wreck our lives. Second, what did Jesus say that we should pray for deliverance from? What is the evil one doing in our lives that has us trapped? Reading all four verses together gives us the answer:

> Forgive us our debts,
> as we also have forgiven our debtors.
> And lead us not into temptation,
> but deliver us from the evil one. For if you forgive men
> when they sin against you, your heavenly Father will
> also forgive you. But if you do not forgive men their
> sins, your Father will not forgive your sins.

Both preceding and following verse 13 is one single word—*forgive*! It occurs six times in this passage, to be exact. The way the evil one keeps us trapped is by coaxing us to live with unforgiving hearts. Jesus could have been envisioning all the different situations we would need deliverance from, but the context makes it clear that an unforgiving heart is specifically what he had in mind here.

Why does the evil one have such a vested interest in keeping us from forgiving those who have hurt us?

Satan hurts God by hurting us. The Bible tells us that Satan's goal is to oppose God and everything he stands for. The problem is that Satan can't hurt God, but he can hurt the closest and most precious thing to him: us. To hurt me, you might hit me, shoot me, or poison me, but as a parent I know that if you really want to devastate me, just hurt one of my children. Satan's strategy is similar—he can't hurt God, so he tries to hurt the closest thing to God, the creatures made in God's image—you and me.

Satan continues to hurt us by keeping us trapped. In Satan's eyes, the only thing better than fostering an environment where people hurt one another is coaxing people who have been hurt to spend the rest of their lives consumed with bitterness and resentment, poisoning everyone and everything they touch.

In his classic fourteenth-century poem *The Inferno*, Dante Alighieri paints a dramatic portrait of the soul's journey through hell. Near the end of his journey, Dante stumbles upon a man named Count Ugolino, cannibalizing the body of Archbishop Ruggieri. The two had been political allies while alive, but at some point Archbishop Ruggieri betrayed Count Ugolino and locked him and his four sons in a tower where they all starved to death. Dante discovers these rivals both in hell, Ugolino gnawing on the archbishop's skull in a picture of eternal bitterness. Upon discovering the gruesome scene, Dante says, "That sinner raised his mouth from his fierce meal, then used the head that he had ripped apart in back: he wiped his lips upon its hair."[2]

That's Satan's plan—crafting an environment where people spend their entire lives trapped, consumed, and filled with vengeful thoughts and feelings of hatred. Do you really want to live like that?

Satan's Main Weapon Is Deceit

The evil one's main weapon in his effort to keep us trapped inside unforgiving hearts is not floating shoes, red eyes staring back at us in our mirrors, or heads spinning around like in *The Exorcist*. If only his strategy were that obvious! Satan's main weapon is deceit. Jesus said the devil is "a liar and the father of lies" (John 8:44). His main strategy is to keep us believing lies that will keep us from getting rid of the gorilla, and one of the biggest is the lie that our struggle with an unforgiving heart is purely a psychological problem.

Forgiving those who hurt us only begins when we are able to answer one simple question: Is the gorilla a psychological problem to be diagnosed and treated with the latest therapeutic insights or techniques, or is it a spiritual problem to be addressed through uniquely spiritual answers taught in the Bible?

Until I met Kathy, my answer had been "Both." But to be perfectly honest, until that day, the more I read Christian books on forgiveness, the more I began to view ancient spiritual practices from Scripture as more the obligatory surface solution to my problem, while the latest psychological insights and techniques remained my real hope for a deep, lasting cure.

My understanding of the role psychology plays in the forgiveness process reminds me of something that happened on a school night a few years ago. We were running behind; it was 5:55, and we had to be at my oldest daughter Kelsey's parent-teacher conference by 6:30. Dinner wasn't on the table (I think it was my night to cook), so we stopped at a local pizza shop around the corner from our house.

As I stood in line, I couldn't make up my mind. Slice of cheese with barbeque chicken? Slice of vegetable with gorgonzola? Ham and pineapple? *Man, pizza sure has changed since I was a kid*, I thought. Pressed for time, I told the guy at the counter, "I'll take that dish over there with the chicken and broccoli and white stuff sprinkled all over it."

When the waitress dropped off our food at our table, we said a quick prayer and dove in. "We're out of here in ten minutes," I said.

To my surprise the white stuff turned out to be freshly ground garlic, which was fantastic. With my mouth full, I shouted to no one in particular, "Dis stuff is gwate!" and proceeded to devour the entire bowl. Twenty minutes later, we were briskly walking into the school building with only moments to spare.

As I held the door open for my family, Chandler, my middle daughter, caught a whiff of my breath. "Dad, you stink," she said.

"I do not."

"Yes you do!"

"It's horrible," Lisa added, pinching her nose.

"Come here," I said to Camryn, my youngest. "I know you'll tell me the truth." I breathed into her face and said, "Shoot me straight."

She threw her hand over her mouth and said, "I'm going to barf."

I panicked. I was just moments away from sitting face-to-face with my daughter's teachers. I rummaged through Lisa's purse, grabbed a piece of gum, and headed for the bathroom. Once inside I took a handful of toilet paper, scrubbed my tongue, and threw the piece of gum in my mouth. Then I began wildly licking my hands and wiping the gum juice all over my face. Once I was done, I took a deep breath, winked at myself in the mirror, and said, "That'll take care of it."

I won't bore you with the details—one teacher covering her mouth with her hand, the other purposely scooting his chair backward, my daughter's hopes of getting into Harvard dashed, subsequent marriage counseling, etc. It was ugly. The smell was so bad it stayed with me well into the following day.

I shared this story with a doctor in our church who told me that the gum treated only part of the problem; the odor wasn't coming just from my mouth. Garlic, he explained, is expunged through the pores as you sweat, as well as through the mouth. I couldn't have contained all the smell no matter what I tried.

The reason so many of us who struggle with the gorilla have failed to eradicate him from our lives isn't for lack of understanding the psychological realities involved in the process of forgiving. More than likely, we've read a few books, watched some self-help television shows, and maybe even sat down with a professional counselor. Those things can be helpful, especially the counseling, but if that's all we rely upon, it's like rubbing gum juice on the problem—over time we realize that the core issue is still with us.

The real reason we have such a hard time forgiving is because we grew up in a loveless family. It's because while everyone else in our neighborhood had a dad who loved them unconditionally, ours drank. It's because our husbands cheated on us. It's because our daughter was taken from us by a drunk driver. It's because we carry around emotional wounds that feel like someone slapped a hand grenade in our gut and walked away. And while a great therapist can be indispensable for understanding why we're empty and broken and mad at everyone in the world including ourselves, there's nothing that a therapist or the latest psychological insight can do to actually fill the void.

Forgiveness is first and foremost a spiritual issue, and in the remaining chapters of this book we'll look at the uniquely spiritual activities the Bible tells us to engage in that enable us to get rid of the gorilla. Oddly enough, these ancient spiritual practices have absolutely nothing at all to do with the devil and everything to do with recklessly throwing our hearts out in front of the oncoming grace of God.

As an outreach-focused church, Christ's Church of the Valley tends to draw people who have very little experience in church and next to no biblical knowledge at all. From time to time, a visitor will request to sit down with me to talk about a personal issue that he or she is struggling with. Most of the time, the topic of forgiveness will come up at some point in the discussion, and often I'll share Kathy's story. At least half of the people who hear it look at me with a blank expression and say, "Look, that's a nice story and all, but I don't know if I believe in God, let alone the devil."

When that happens, I say, "That's unfortunate."

"Why?" they ask.

"Because that might explain why you're having such a hard time with forgiveness."

GETTING RID
OF THE GORILLA

7

CALL

In Argentina we sometimes use this baptismal formula: "I kill you in the name of the Father, and of the Son, and of the Holy Spirit, and I make you born into the Kingdom of God to serve Him and to please Him." It's different, but it works much better.

—Juan Carlos Ortiz

Years ago when my family and I moved to the suburbs of Philadelphia to start Christ's Church of the Valley, I quickly realized that we had landed in an immensely wealthy area. This concerned me for two reasons. First, Jesus warned that it is extremely difficult to make authentic Christ followers out of the rich. Second, I knew my own heart. I knew I had the potential to be lured away by the seduction of affluence just like anyone else.

So I decided to make a statement about the values of this new church before we even had our first public service. I did something that many Christians would consider strange: I took every penny in our church's checking account (it wasn't much) and blew it all in one day on the poor. I wanted the first dollar spent by our church to make a statement about the kind of church we were going to become.

I called the local police station and asked, "Where is the most dangerous, drug-infested, crime-ridden neighborhood in our entire region?" Without hesitation, the officer who answered the phone named a neighborhood twenty-five minutes away. "I'm pretty sure we send a car there every night," he said. "Why do you want to know?"

"Well, I'm a Christian, and I want to show people God's love in a tangible way," I replied, "so I thought I would buy groceries for the entire neighborhood."

His response was interesting. "Why the %!@+% would you want to do that? I wouldn't go there without a gun. Knock yourself out."

In a move that would make any marriage counselor proud, I pulled out of the driveway that morning without telling my wife where I was headed. I figured she would worry too much or might think I was crazy. Trust me—there's ghetto, and then there's Philly ghetto. Nevertheless I drove up to a wholesale grocery outlet and filled every inch of my van with boxes of groceries, each with enough food to feed a family of four for a week. The whole time I had this vision of Lisa wondering where I was and then seeing me on the nightly news with a sheet over my body.

You can imagine what I saw when I arrived in the infamous neighborhood. It was like a scene from a war-torn country: broken windows, graffiti everywhere, trash throughout the streets, cars on blocks, people passed out on the sidewalk. And there stood this goofy-looking suburban guy with his arms full of pancake mix and peanut butter. I was petrified. (I'm a chicken, remember?)

"OK, God," I prayed as I knocked on the first door. "Work through me, your chicken." Seconds later a woman carrying a baby came to the door.

"Hi, my name is Brian, and I'm the pastor of a new church. I wanted to show you God's love in a practical way. Do you need any groceries?"

"What church are you from?"

"Um, well, that's a great question! We don't have a name yet."

"And you want to give me groceries? For free?"

"Yep. And maybe a quick prayer."

She slammed the door right in my face. *Well, this is going great,* I thought. In a few seconds, the door reopened. "OK, I guess." The woman had a smile on her face. I smiled right back at her, carried the food into her barren apartment, and then put my arms around her and her baby and prayed for them.

A man popped his head inside her door and asked, "What's going on here?" I explained what I was doing and ended up praying for him too. Few times have I ever prayed for so many hurting people in one day. I prayed for a prostitute, then a drug addict, then a guard at the local penitentiary who was sleeping on the floor of his apartment, then for at least a dozen or so others. These people had nothing. Zilch. As I moved slowly through the neighborhood, I touched and hugged and prayed for as many people as I could.

When I finally got back into my empty van, instead of feeling a sense of joy, I recalled my earlier conversation with the police officer and got angry. Why would that cop be so surprised that a Christian would want to do something like this? Why is it that people have grown to expect so little out of Christians? That word, *Christian*, has become as tantalizing as a warm Coke at a summer picnic.

THE PROBLEM WITH "CHRISTIAN"

Despite its wide use in our culture, the word *Christian* is not used much in the Bible; in fact, it only occurs three times![1] It never crossed Jesus' lips. Paul never used it. It did not originate as a word believers used to describe themselves. Acts 11:26 says, "The disciples were called Christians first at Antioch." By whom?—the unbelievers in Antioch. *Christian* comes from the Greek word *Christianos,* which means "belonging to, identified with, or adherents or followers of Christ."[2]

Another difficulty with *Christian* is that our market-driven culture has taken it hostage. Rather than being a term that might evoke hostility and persecution, as Jesus said might happen to his followers, *Christian* has become a corporate marketing niche. *Christian* offends no one. In America we have Christian paraphernalia galore. We have Christian bookstores, Christian television stations, and Christian websites. Those who are curious can flip through a Christian best seller, thumb through a multitude of Christian magazines, or sit back and enjoy a blockbuster Christian motion picture. One can quickly find Christian solutions for any and every problem a bewildered American faces—there are Christian exercise videos, Christian weight-loss programs, and now even Christian vitamins.

My biggest problem with the word *Christian*, however, is that it doesn't capture what a Christ follower *does*. I like titles that are behaviorally descriptive. A baseball player plays baseball. A stockbroker buys and sells company stock. The word *Christian* tells us who we belong to but not what we do. It isn't an action word. It doesn't carry an inherent job description or an implied set of behavioral expectations.

It communicates that we belong to Christ, a solid idea in and of itself but one that has lost its edge in our culture.

A MORE POTENT WORD

Let me reacquaint you with an old, out-of-date, and often misunderstood word: *disciple*. In my mind, replacing *Christian* with *disciple* is key to getting rid of the gorilla. In fact, from now on, I want to challenge you to use the word *disciple* every time you are about to say *Christian*.

At first it will seem a little awkward. Your neighbors might think you've joined some strange chicken-sacrificing cult, but that's precisely the point. Jim Jones and Charles Manson stole the word *disciple* from us. We're stealing it back.

Go on, try it. Say out loud, "I'm glad I'm a Christian."

Now try, "I'm glad I'm a disciple."

Disciple occurs not three times but over two hundred sixty times throughout the pages of the New Testament. As philosopher Dallas Willard has said, "The New Testament is a book about disciples, by disciples, and for disciples of Jesus."[3] Derived from the Greek word *mathetes*, which means "learner" or "pupil,"[4] a disciple is simply one who learns from a teacher. But Jesus expanded this meaning. According to Jesus, our mission on earth is not only to create Christ followers who know his teachings but also who obey his teachings. Jesus said, "All authority in heaven and on earth has been given to me. Therefore go and make disciples of all nations, baptizing them in the name of the Father and of the Son and of the Holy Spirit, and teaching them to obey everything I have commanded you. And surely I am with you always, to the very end of the age" (Matthew 28:18-20).

According to Jesus, a disciple has one simple job in life: to learn and obey what Jesus taught. Today, however, we tend to communicate "First you become a Christian, and after that you can work at becoming a disciple." We mistakenly allow the impression that obeying Jesus is something that can be put off until later, like dieting or changing the oil in the car. Discipleship is treated like honors courses in high school: they're not essential for graduation but you can take them if you want to. Yet Jesus said that discipleship begins at conversion. Trusting him to forgive our sins and getting baptized are simply our first steps in a lifetime of discipleship. When believers are called *disciples*, life change is expected. Transformation is an assumed part of the journey from the beginning. Sadly, our culture has caught on to the fact that there is virtually no difference between the way Christians live compared to the general public. Should we be surprised? We are simply reaping what one author calls "the cost of nondiscipleship."[5]

A few years ago, I was driving in center city Philadelphia and got lost, a common occurrence for me. Without knowing it, I pulled onto a narrow, one-way road. Cars started barreling toward me. Horns were blaring. Cars were pulling out of my way. People motioned for me to go back the other way and said things I can't repeat in this book. It reminded me of that bumper sticker, "If you don't like the way I drive, stay off the sidewalk."

Say what you want about my navigational ability—there wasn't a person on that street who didn't know (A) that I was there and (B) which direction I was headed. That's what happens when Christians become disciples.

People notice disciples. Disciples do not blend in very easily. Disciples do not just believe differently, they behave differently. They stick out. They provoke. They cause people to think. Disciples jar others to evaluate their own lives, often without uttering a word. Disciples point people to the kingdom of God simply by their behavior alone.

THE POWERFUL IMAGE OF BAPTISM

People living in the U.S. in the twenty-first century are pampered beyond imagination. Our market-driven consumer economy is powered by the quest to find out what makes people happy so they'll part with their money and buy XYZ Company's products. Every day we are bombarded with countless marketing messages and told that our needs, our desires, and our wishes are supreme.

That's why I love the powerful image of baptism. One of the most countercultural acts around is a believer getting baptized as a response to Jesus' call to discipleship. In fact, I love inviting spiritual inquirers to observe our baptism services. But watching someone get baptized can be unnerving.

One reason baptism disturbs us is it's a little odd. If you've ever seen a baptism, admit it—it is a strange thing to watch. One day a guy is putting with his buddy Harry on the sixteenth hole of the neighborhood golf course, and the next day some nutty religious group is dunking him under water.

Baptism is also humbling. No one can baptize himself. Everyone gets wet; no exceptions. Cell phones, luxury cars, expensive homes, stock options—none of these matter. Baptism makes everyone equal.

The image of baptism is most unnerving, however, when we finally get what it means to be a disciple. Nothing in our faith so powerfully conveys the countercultural redirection of a life like a person being baptized. Baptism is the ritual that tells an unbelieving world we're slamming on the brakes with both feet, wildly swerving the car around, and heading the "wrong way" up a one-way cultural street.

Jesus said that the very first thing we are to do when helping people become disciples is to immerse them (Matthew 28:19). That's what *baptism* means. The Greek word *baptizo* means "dip," "immerse," or "submerge."⁶ Why did Jesus pick immersion as the initiation rite for becoming his follower? What was he trying to convey with this image? Romans 6 makes it clear that one of the primary pictures Jesus had in mind was decomposition—baptism is actually a mock tomb.

When we are lowered into the water, it is as if we are being lowered into a grave. Being raised up out of the water symbolizes that just as Jesus was raised from the dead, we too are raised to live a completely different life. God is saying through the image of baptism, "Let me clarify something from the very beginning. This whole journey is about death. Death to yourself. Death to the culture in which you live. Death to your hatred. Death to your revenge. Death to your ambitions, your dreams, your wishes, your everything. But it's also about life! My life within you. My life to work in and through and around you to accomplish my will on this earth."

ASK THE RIGHT QUESTION

One of the things you must understand if you are ever going to get rid of the gorilla is this: before Jesus ever calls you to forgive, he calls you to be his disciple. If you really want to forgive someone but can't, then maybe forgiveness *isn't* what you're struggling with. Maybe your fight is with what has to be done *before* forgiveness can truly happen. For some of us, maybe getting rid of the gorilla is not about forgiveness at all but about deciding whether to answer Jesus' call to discipleship.

No one who reads the Gospels walks away with the impression that following Jesus will be easy. Take a look at the following statements Jesus made about his expectations for the way his disciples would treat one another:

> Then Peter came to Jesus and asked, "Lord, how many times shall I forgive my brother when he sins against me? Up to seven times?" Jesus answered, "I tell you, not seven times, but seventy-seven times" (Matthew 18:21, 22).

> If your brother sins, rebuke him, and if he repents, forgive him. If he sins against you seven times in a day, and seven times comes back to you and says, "I repent," forgive him (Luke 17:3, 4).

The lavishness with which Jesus calls us to forgive one another is nothing short of astonishing, but it is nothing compared to his request that we forgive our bitter enemies:

> You have heard that it was said, "Love your neighbor and hate your enemy." But I tell you: Love your enemies and pray for those who persecute you (Matthew 5:43, 44).

You might read these verses of Scripture and wonder, *Could I ever do that?* If so, you're asking the wrong question.

I don't know if I could ever go into combat. I see the images on television—the firefights, the bravery, the sacrifices, the casualties—

and I wonder if I have what it takes. The first and hardest decision, however, is not whether I could jump into a firefight with an AK-47, but whether I could join the military in the first place. If I reach the point where I feel called to enter the military and I sign the papers, then at that point I've already decided that I am willing to go into battle. Answering yes to the first question, Can I serve in the military? automatically answers the second, Can I go into combat?

Forgiveness works the same way. When we look at the requirements—forgiving fellow disciples without limit, forgiving anyone who causes us harm—we rightfully ask, Could I really do that? but that's the wrong question to *focus* on. Can I answer Jesus' call to discipleship? is the first and most important question. If we answer that affirmatively, we automatically answer, Can I forgive?

We forgive not because we want to, or because it improves our lives, or because we're sick of living with the aftereffects of not doing so; we forgive because that's what disciples do. Disciples obey Jesus, and Jesus teaches us to forgive other people when they hurt us. So we forgive them—immediately, completely, and without reservation. As disciples, because we've already decided up front that we'll obey Jesus' commands, the question now is not will we forgive, but how?

Of course, if forgiveness always happened easily and quickly, then I wouldn't be writing this book, and you wouldn't be reading it.

For years I felt like a hypocrite. I struggled with the fact that I say I'm a disciple, one who obeys Christ's commands, but inwardly I disobey his command to forgive; I harbor ill feeling toward those who have hurt me. My inability to get rid of the gorilla has caused me, at times, to doubt that I'm a genuine follower of Christ.

Then I learned a simple little prayer, one of the most biblical, godly, Christ-honoring prayers I know.

If you've already answered Jesus' call to discipleship and are having trouble forgiving those who hurt you, that doesn't mean you aren't a genuine follower of Jesus. You simply need him to teach you how to obey his command to forgive. Every disciple on the planet is in a process of learning to obey Jesus' commands. No one becomes a disciple and instantly becomes 100 percent obedient. Forgiveness just happens to be the one command you and I need a little more one-on-one time with the Teacher to finally get right. The little prayer I learned will remind you of this. In fact, the rest of this book looks at how we place ourselves in a position to allow Jesus to answer it.

Here's the prayer: "Jesus, I hate this person. Teach me how to love and forgive him."

8

KINDNESS

*When you see your enemy and yourself in the weakness
and silliness of the humanity you share, you will make the
miracle of forgiving a little easier.*

—LEWIS SMEDES

My earliest memory in life is of my parents throwing rolls of toilet paper into the branches of the oak tree in my grandparents' front yard. I believe I was three at the time. I remember just standing there, slightly bewildered, not quite sure what to make of my parents—both in their late twenties, running, laughing, and smiling like two mischievous teenagers who had snuck out to play a late-night prank on a friend.

Off to my left my grandfather stood on the porch, a man of solid stature, hands on his hips, head shaking back and forth, a slight smile on his face. I remember his thick-rimmed glasses and his crew cut, greased back and parted to the side—later on my high school geometry teacher, Mr. Tykoti, wore his hair the same way.

That's my earliest memory in life, and unfortunately it's also the only memory I have of my grandfather; he died of a heart attack soon after, at fifty-six.

I'm always intrigued by what our minds choose to recall. For instance, I'm puzzled by the fact that while I can remember my grandfather standing on his porch, I have no recollection of a memorial service, or a car ride to the cemetery, or people crying, a minister reading Scripture, the family gathering at the church afterward to eat and stand around and talk—everything I grew to expect later in life when other family members passed away. The only memory I have of my grandfather is toilet paper and an awkward smile. A few years ago I asked my parents what in the world they were doing that day. They said it was my grandparents' anniversary.

While I have only one memory of my grandfather, my dad shaped nearly everything about me as a man. In fact, he was so influential that all my friends gravitated to my house to hang out when we were growing up. For a while I thought they just liked hanging out with me, but over time it became apparent they were coming over to be around my dad. Strong, positive, consistent, and generous, he was the kind of father most of my friends wished they had. He became sort of a second father to a lot of them, something I never resented. My parents were always special guests at my friends' weddings, even if I wasn't able to attend. Friends dropping by their home with new babies became commonplace.

Years ago when I went to visit my great aunt in the nursing home, I opened the door and asked, "Aunt Pauline, we haven't seen each other in a very long time. Do you remember me?" I'll never forget the pride I felt as she smiled, sat up in her bed, and said in her soft Kentucky accent, "Why, of course I do. You're Charlie's boy."

I don't want you to get the impression that my father was perfect, because he wasn't. While I was in high school, my dad was the coach of our church's softball team, and when the time came to play St. Mary's Catholic Church down the street, he didn't view it as just any old softball game: five hundred years of theological debate was on the line! If we lost to the Catholics, in my dad's mind, it would be as if we were endorsing the crusades or encouraging people to pray to Mary, or—worse—validating playing bingo in church. With the entire Protestant Reformation on the line, my dad did what he knew he had to do: he asked me and a few of my friends on my high school baseball team to come as guest players to trounce 'em.

On one particular day, the St. Mary's team was chosen to provide the umpire. The score was tied in the final inning with bases loaded. My friend Deron stepped up to the plate and hit a rocket to the infield. St. Mary's second baseman, probably on summer break from Notre Dame himself, fired the ball to home plate as our player came barreling toward the base. With the crowd on its feet, tension in the air, the debate over the existence of purgatory on the line, our player slid into home plate, clearly ahead of the ball. The umpire yelled, "You're out!" and St. Mary's won the game. Everyone on our team went nuts! My dad, furious at this seemingly blatant attempt to cheat, ran to home plate, threw his hat down, and screamed, "Are you blind? Come on!" I ran up behind him and said, "Dad, calm down. I think that umpire is their priest."

He wasn't perfect by any stretch, and he still isn't, but my dad's faith and character shaped me in profound ways. I had such a great experience growing up that I assumed that Dad grew up with the kind of father I had, but nothing could be further from the truth. My dad is a great storyteller, and I always thought it odd growing up that I never heard him talk very much about his own father. As

I would learn late in my twenties, sometimes there are stories that are better left untold.

One morning my dad, my two sisters, and I went out to eat, and the subject of our childhoods came up. At some point in the conversation, one of us joked about how tough growing up in the Jones household was, and then, for some reason, I asked Dad what my grandfather had been like.

"He was fine."

"No, seriously," I shot back. "You never talk about him. I don't know anything about him. I want to know what he was like."

Sensing that the time had come, Dad wiped his mouth with his napkin, set it on his lap, and then upended everything we thought we knew about his childhood. He began by telling us that his father didn't take care of the family real well; he had a gambling problem. Oftentimes if it weren't for the generosity of family members, there wouldn't have been anything to eat. My grandfather's card playing was a mixed blessing, though, because at least when he was out with his friends after work, he wasn't home hitting his wife, my grandmother, a tiny thing, barely five feet tall, thin, soft-spoken, and gentle.

James Baldwin wrote, "Man does not remember the hand that struck him, the darkness that frightened him, as a child; nevertheless, the hand and the darkness remain with him, indivisible from himself forever, part of the passion that drives him."[1] As Dad talked, shades of his personality began to make sense to me; reasons for the way he behaved and made decisions, invisible up to that point, began to come clear. I began to understand why I can recall my dad becoming upset with my mom only one time while I was growing up, just one time. I'm sure they fought, just never in front of us. I began to understand why I've never seen my dad drink. Once when I was young, someone gave my parents a very expensive bottle of wine as a gift. When the guest was gone, my dad threw the unopened bottle in the trash. I began to understand why when Lisa and I lived in New Jersey, visiting Atlantic City never appealed to him.

If the neglect and physical abuse weren't enough, when my dad was in the fourth or fifth grade his father abducted him and his older brother and moved to northern Ohio for an entire year. Family members on my grandfather's side knew where they went but wouldn't tell my frantic and grief-stricken grandmother. My dad said while his father went to work and his older brother went to school, he was forced to stay home by himself the entire school year, locked in the house. Eventually they returned to Kentucky.

"Did he change when you guys moved back?" my sister asked.

"Not really. Things never really changed until my brother Bob was old enough to stop it. When Bob turned sixteen, he ran into the kitchen late one night as they were fighting. Bob told him if he ever laid a hand on her again, he'd kill him. He never touched her again."

With that last piece of information, Dad picked up his fork and took another bite of his eggs. Never again have I heard him speak another word about his father's shortcomings. Since then, however, he has made sure we've learned about the positive aspects of my grandfather's life, like the way he mellowed when my oldest sister was born, or the fact that he was one of the first people in our entire family to graduate from college. I've learned that my dad, his two brothers, and my grandfather couldn't talk about much, but they all shared a fanatical interest in University of Kentucky basketball and talking about new cars. My dad would be the first to say that he would have loved seeing who my grandfather might have become with God's help if his life hadn't been tragically cut short.

Chances are you're having a hard time forgiving your father too. Or maybe it is your wife, or someone in your church. It might even be some random person you met on the street who upended your life in a split-second encounter. It could be there's really no one in particular that you're angry with. Maybe you've just allowed yourself to become the kind of person for whom handing out second chances is a difficult proposition. If so, there's a reason I'm sharing my father's story.

Knowing what I know now, I look back on my earliest memory in life very differently. There stands my dad, toilet paper in hand, kids in tow, a father in his late twenties, just old enough to begin to understand and feel the emotional fallout of growing up with an unhealthy parent. As he covers the yard with toilet paper, his father stands off to the side on the porch with an awkward smile, knowing full well that most children would have disowned him after what he did.

My grandfather made horrendous choices, went out carousing, gambled away his paychecks as his kids went hungry, chose to hurt his wife, and robbed my dad of a lifetime of great memories and experiences. Yet, despite everything that had happened up to that point, because he was a disciple something inside pushed my dad to get out of bed that morning, grab some toilet paper, put his family in the car, and go do something completely unnatural and undeserved—he chose to show my grandfather kindness.

And it's that kind of act, a simple display of unvarnished grace, that is going to be the way out of this emotional prison we find ourselves in. First Peter 3:9 tells us, "Do not repay evil with evil or insult with insult, but with blessing, because to this you were called so that you may inherit a blessing." Hatred is what has imprisoned us. Kindness is our ticket out. We've got to do what disciples do. Disciples love their enemies, personal enemies with names and faces and horrible parenting skills. This is nothing new. Disciples have been doing this for two thousand years of history. What we have to understand is that showing kindness to our enemies is essential to kicking the gorilla out of our lives for good. Let me share two important reasons why.

A SOFTENING AGENT FOR OUR HEARTS

It's hard to imagine what life must have been like more than thirty-five hundred years ago. No running water. No electricity. No refrigerators. No Chick-fil-A sandwiches with that little pickle on the bottom. I couldn't have done it. I think the hardest part of life back then, besides the horrible living conditions, must have been the violence. Historians point to examples in the ancient world of governments that did a good job maintaining justice and civil order for its citizens. Yet, as spectacular as these countries were, leaving behind a vast array of literary works and archaeological wonders, the vast majority of people alive at the time lived just outside their reach. Their daily lives were anything but civilized.

Over three millennia ago, most of the people on this planet lived under the rule of brutal thugs and warlords. Women and children were considered property with no rights of their own, often brutalized and killed at whim. I have a friend who is a pastor in Nairobi, Kenya, and he tells me that the various world health organizations estimate that in the slums where he works, up to 80 percent of the women use their bodies to pay for food and basic necessities for their children. We have no such statistics from the ancient world, but one can only imagine how women, children, the weak and oppressed were treated at the time. A quick reading of the book of Joshua in the Old Testament gives us a tiny window into how brutal the world was during the building of the nation of Israel. Just imagine what it was like before God's people showed up.

When God called Israel into existence and gave them rules to guide their lives, one of the most countercultural commandments he gave is found in Leviticus 24:17-20:

> If anyone takes the life of a human being, he must be put
> to death. Anyone who takes the life of someone's animal
> must make restitution—life for life. If anyone injures his
> neighbor, whatever he has done must be done to him:
> fracture for fracture, eye for eye, tooth for tooth. As he
> has injured the other, so he is to be injured.

At first glance, it doesn't seem much different from what we've been describing, especially when we read the word *must* next to "put to death," but it represented a major shift in how people were to treat one another. What God did was put into place a limit on how much people could retaliate when they were hurt. No longer could an Israelite whose leg was accidentally maimed go out and lynch the man who did it along with his wife, children, and entire extended family. If justice needed to be handed out, it was to be limited to an action proportionate to the crime (for example, maiming the other person's leg).

That commandment provided an outlet for retaliation while maintaining social and civil order, but it wasn't intended to heal broken hearts—justice can never do that.

The other day I was watching the news and a young woman was being interviewed outside a courtroom. Years ago her father was senselessly murdered outside a mom and pop grocery store in Philly, and the killer had finally been sentenced to death row—an eye for an eye. Was there relief when the killer was read his sentence at the trial? Absolutely. Will that relief last? We all know the answer to that. The punishment, while proportionate to the crime and necessary to satisfy the need for justice, unfortunately won't give that woman her dad back. It won't make any difference on her wedding day when he should be walking her down the aisle. It won't make any difference when her firstborn child grows old enough to start asking questions about his or her grandfather. Justice, while necessary for civil order, can't change what's already been done. It can't bring people back, and it definitely can't get rid of the gorilla.

The only thing that can begin to heal the heart is what Jesus taught in Matthew 5:38-42:

> You have heard that it was said, "Eye for eye, and tooth for tooth." But I tell you, Do not resist an evil person. If someone strikes you on the right cheek, turn to him the other also. And if someone wants to sue you and take your tunic, let him have your cloak as well. If someone forces you to go one mile, go with him two miles. Give to the one who asks you, and do not turn away from the one who wants to borrow from you.

We read that, and at first glance we wonder how that's going to make anything better. Not only aren't we allowed to get back at people, but Jesus allows for no retaliation at all. In fact, Jesus' command doesn't take the Old Testament "eye for an eye" law just one step further, but two. Not only are we not allowed to retaliate, but choosing to do nothing after we've been hurt isn't allowed either. According to Jesus, when we're hurt we are to return kindness for pain, blessing for cursing, and toilet paper for neglect.

His reason is simple: showing kindness does something mystical to us. Seeing our kindness in action hopefully draws the person who hurt us closer to God, but I don't think that's the primary reason Jesus gave us this command. Instead, we're to show kindness because doing so forces us into the flow of the Spirit. It forces us to do what only God—or God's Spirit in us—is capable of doing. First Peter 3:9 tells us that we receive a blessing when we display kindness. That blessing is the unexpected way we feel something again—a spiritual flicker, a faint sensation in our hearts that goes out to that person, an incomprehensible touch of empathy. I'm not sure exactly what it is, but I know something happens. I've felt it, and if you can find the will to display kindness to the person who has hurt you, I promise you'll feel it too.

If I were to make a list of the hardest things in life to forgive, near the top of the list would have to be forgiving your husband or wife for having an affair. In all my years of being a pastor, I've found few situations as excruciating as helping someone find the strength to forgive a wayward spouse. Years ago I had a chance to help a friend after she discovered that her husband had initiated an affair with someone in his office. I thought it odd at the time that what my friend couldn't get over wasn't so much the sexual aspect of her husband's relationship with the other woman but the way he was totally smitten by her. Brazen, unrepentant, and giddier than a twelve-year-old passing love notes under his desk, her husband flaunted his feelings for the other woman in his wife's face.

She tried counseling and group therapy, but nothing helped. Twice they got back together, but both times her husband went right back to his affair. His inability to shut his feelings down for this other woman reminds me of Philip, the main character in Somerset Maugham's classic book *Of Human Bondage*. Philip had fallen in love with a barmaid named Mildred and couldn't escape the overwhelming attraction he felt for her. While discussing Philip's inability to stop pursuing her, despite the pitiful way Mildred treated him in return, one of Philip's friends observed:

'You seem to be a contented slave of your passions.'

'A slave because I can't help myself, but not a contented one,' laughed Philip.

While he spoke he thought of that hot madness which had driven him in pursuit of Mildred. He remembered how he had chafed against it and how he had felt the degradation of it.

'Thank God, I'm free from all that now,' he thought.

And yet even as he said it he was not quite sure whether he spoke sincerely. When he was under the influence of passion he had felt a singular vigour, and his mind had worked with unwonted force. He was more alive, there was an excitement in sheer being, an eager vehemence of soul, which made life now a trifle dull. For all the misery he had endured there was compensation in that sense of rushing, overwhelming existence.[2]

Eventually my friend had enough and kicked his rear to the curb, as she should have, and filed for divorce. Yet the divorce only settled living arrangements and rules for sharing custody of their daughter; it didn't settle her heart. She hated him, and rightly so. But the more she hated him the more she mistreated him, and the more she mistreated him the more it affected her daughter. Eventually her daughter's reactions to her behavior reflected back to her what a miserable person she was becoming. She was trapped in a miserable cycle. She stopped caring for herself. She cut herself off from her friends and threw herself into anything that would give her a quick fix, but nothing took her mind off what her husband did to her. Six years later she woke up one day staring nose to nose with the gorilla and knew she had to do something, so she came by to talk.

What I told her is what I want to tell you now: you need to find a way to begin to show kindness to the person who hurt you. He won't deserve it and she probably won't appreciate it, but that's not the point. You're not doing it for the other person anyway, at least not initially. You need to find a way to show that person kindness for one person and one person only: yourself. Showing kindness softens our hearts.

Think for a moment. What's one tangible thing you could do for this person as soon as you get done reading this chapter? For some like my friend, it might be to make a commitment to stop speaking negatively to your children about your former spouse. For others it might mean picking up the phone and calling him on his birthday. Maybe it's forgiving a financial debt, or writing a note to the guy in jail, or smiling the next time you see her. If the person has already passed, maybe you can send some money to a mission as a memorial gift or place flowers on the gravestone. Maybe all you can muster is putting this book down and saying a quick prayer for that person. Whatever it is, do it, because that's what disciples do. Do it even though it's painful and irrational. Do it even though you feel nothing while you do it. Do it out of devotion to Christ. Do it to receive a blessing in return. Do it to get rid of the gorilla. Do it over and over again, and watch what happens.

A REMINDER OF OUR COMMON SINFULNESS

Showing kindness not only softens the heart, it also reminds us of the true condition of our souls. As I wrote about in *Second Guessing God*, one of my children's favorite vacation activities is a game they call "baptize the sinner." It goes something like this: Starting five hundred miles away from our destination, my kids start asking, "Are we there yet?" After Lisa and I answer no two thousand or more times, finally we make it to the hotel. We drag our suitcases to our room, where the kids change into their swimsuits and then make a mad dash for the pool. We'll swim for what seems like hours, and then at some point I'll overhear my middle daughter yell out, "Are you a sinner?" My oldest will yell back, "Yes!" Then my middle one shouts, "Well, be baptized, you sinner, and become a Christian!" and slams her sister into the water like a heavyweight wrestler. Then my youngest will jump up and down and yell, "My turn!" This continues until everyone has been dunked four or five times. When I first saw my girls playing like this, I told my wife, "This is blasphemy." She laughed and asked, "What kind of games do you expect pastors' kids to play?"

We don't use the word *sinner* much anymore, which is odd, because as disciples of Christ it's one of the few things we have in common with one another. Think about it. If we both belong to a country club, what do we have in common? Not much other than the fact that we both like golf and can afford the expensive dues to join. If we both join the local VFW, what do we have in common? We're both veterans of foreign wars. If we both join the church, what do we have in common? We're both sinners. Admitting our sinfulness is *the* requirement for entry into the kingdom of God. Matthew tells us that the first words out of Jesus' mouth when he began recruiting people to join him were "Repent, for the kingdom of heaven is near" (Matthew 4:17). When God brought about the birth of the church and people asked about the entry requirements, Peter replied, "Repent and be baptized, every one of you, in the name of Jesus Christ for the forgiveness of your sins" (Acts 2:38).

Ironically, when someone hurts us, usually the first thing we forget is our own sinfulness. That's understandable. When we're hurt, it's hard to focus on anything but the other person's faults. We analyze those to death, picking the person apart in our minds and keeping meticulous mental notes of faults and weaknesses. It's an understandable trap to fall into, because when we are hurt we do need to step back and analyze the situation to see how we should respond appropriately. However, most of us stay in that posture a little too long, and over time we become comfortable viewing life from that vantage point. The problem is that if all we do is focus on our own pain and the other person's faults, we end up blinding ourselves to the reality of our own condition. We begin looking much better than we actually are. We overlook faults of our own. Someone once said that in times of war the first casualty is truth. I don't know much about war, but I've spent a lot of time with the gorilla, and when someone wrestles with an unforgiving heart, the first casualty usually is repentance. Oswald Chambers observed, "Repentance does not bring a sense of sin, but a sense of unutterable unworthiness. When I repent, I realize that I am utterly helpless; I know all through me that I am not worthy even to bear His shoes. Have I repented like that? Or is there a lingering suggestion of standing up for myself? The reason God cannot come into my life is because I am not through into repentance."[3]

The reality is you may be in more pain than the person who hurt you, and that person might be completely to blame for your predicament. But never forget this: you are not more moral than that person, no matter how deeply he or she hurt you. Romans 3:23 reminds us, "All have sinned and fall short of the glory of God." That includes you and the person who hurt you. Repentance means that we acknowledge before God that we are no better than anyone else and that we are only followers of Christ because of God's limitless mercy and forgiveness. Colossians 3:13 exhorts us, "Forgive as the Lord forgave you." Maybe the reason we have such a hard time with the command to forgive is that we have a bad memory. Maybe our difficulty isn't so much with the desire to forgive but the humility to acknowledge who we really are in the eyes of God.

Those of us who struggle with an unforgiving heart end up comparing ourselves to the wrong person. One day a few years ago, when I went to the gym to work out I didn't have much time, so I decided just to walk a few miles. As I approached the two-lane track, I noticed an elderly woman jump on ahead of me. The way the track operated, walkers used the inside lane and runners used the outside. That day there was a stream of runners jogging really fast, so I'd need to be cautious if I wanted to pass another walker.

I stretched my arms and moved my head side to side as I slowly took a few warm-up laps. Increasing speed, I edged closer and closer to this elderly lady in the walker's lane in front of me, a woman at least in her eighties, profoundly bent over and clearly suffering from an extreme case of osteoporosis. Since I was just warming up, I thought I'd let her go for a while before I'd pass her. Just then she looked back to see where I was, and then, humorously, increased her speed to keep in front of me.

Cute, I thought as I backed off and stayed a few steps behind her.

Soon I was ready to do some serious huffing and puffing, so I sped up and got right on her heels and looked for the next opportunity to pass her. But as I did, she looked back at me and then lunged forward and turned on the burners.

I can't believe this! I thought. So I sped up again and tried to pass her, but she sped up even more. Dozens of runners were blowing right past us on the outside lane, so I was stuck with her in front of me. I tried one more time, but she looked back at me with a nasty glare and sped up even more.

I started getting tired of this. I wanted to exercise and had a lot else to do that day, so I decided to take her at the next curve.

All right, old woman, I thought to myself, *get ready to eat my dust.*

As she turned around once more, I gave her a glare she'd never forget and turned it on full throttle. I opened it up, baby—my head was pointed straight up, the veins on my neck were popping out, my arms were pumping. Cruising along, I saw my opening at the next curve. I looked behind me, saw the gap in the runners' group, quickly made my move into the outside lane, and then blew right past her. I looked back and made a face that proudly said, "Take that, old woman. That's what you get when you mess with the pastor of disaster!"

Once I turned the corner, however, my expression changed as I saw her hobbling behind me. I had gotten so caught up in the moment that I managed to blow past a woman who was older than my grandmother!

The same thing happens when someone hurts us. We get caught up in the emotional aftermath of our pain and forget that the yardstick for moral comparison is not the person who hurt us but God himself. Of course we're going to appear more moral to ourselves than the gossip who hurt us or the boss who mistreated us. They hurt us! How can we not initially react this way? Pain causes people to lose objectivity. We're always going to seem more moral in our own eyes than the person who hurt us.

The Old Testament records that when the prophet Isaiah received his calling, God peeled back the veil that had been shielding Isaiah's eyes from seeing who God was in all of his majesty and power. Isaiah 6:1-4 paints the vision:

> In the year that King Uzziah died, I saw the Lord seated
> on a throne, high and exalted, and the train of his robe
> filled the temple. Above him were seraphs, each with six
> wings: With two wings they covered their faces, with
> two they covered their feet, and with two they were fly-
> ing. And they were calling to one another:

"Holy, holy, holy is the LORD Almighty;
the whole earth is full of his glory."

At the sound of their voices the doorposts and thresh-
olds shook and the temple was filled with smoke.

For the first time in his life, as much as his limited, natural mind could comprehend, Isaiah had a clear picture of who God is. Isaiah came face-to-face with God in the throne room of heaven and understood that what really separated himself from the creator was not his inability to see but his inability to be pure. His reaction is telling—he became completely unraveled by the experience.

As the angels flew around the throne, they cried three times, "Holy, holy, holy." In chapter three I mentioned that ancient Hebrew had no punctuation, so if something was to be emphasized it was either placed at the beginning of a sentence or it was repeated. If it was repeated three times, it was important beyond measure. Every time in the Bible where someone encounters an angel, he or she cowered in fear at their raw beauty and power. Here the angels flew—majestic, supernatural, and awe-inspiring—covering every part of their bodies with their wings in reverence and proclaiming with every ounce of strength they had that God isn't just holy, or doubly holy, but holy beyond comprehension. Isaiah's response was immediate: "'Woe to me!' I cried. 'I am ruined! For I am a man of unclean lips, and I live among a people of unclean lips, and my eyes have seen the King, the LORD Almighty'" (v. 5).

In biblical times if a prophet was to announce a positive word from the Lord, he began his pronouncement with the word *blessed*.

But if a prophet had a message of destruction, he prefaced his word from the Lord with the word *woe*. In the face of God's holiness and utter purity, Isaiah became instantly aware of his own sinfulness and pronounced a curse of destruction upon himself. Isaiah's vision of God gave him a clear understanding of himself, and that's something those of us who wrestle with an unforgiving heart have lost somewhere along the way.

Chances are God's not going to peel back the heavens and give us the same kind of vision he gave Isaiah. He doesn't have to. In its place he's given us the command to show kindness, and in that act God allows us in some mysterious way to see ourselves as Isaiah saw himself. When we extend kindness to those who hurt us, we force ourselves to come to terms with the fact that they don't deserve it but neither do we. Through kindness we grant others the gift of being broken humans, fraught with sinfulness and in need of redemption, free from condemnation. At some point in that exchange—maybe not the first time, maybe not the tenth—we begin to realize that the person who hurt us isn't quite the hideous creature we've painted him out to be and that we're not quite as holy as we've painted ourselves. At some point we realize that the person we just toilet papered shares the same humanity we share and needs the same Savior we need. When we reach that point, the process of forgiveness has already begun.

As Thomas à Kempis said in his spiritual classic *The Imitation of Christ*, "Should you see another person openly doing evil, or carrying out a wicked purpose, do not on that account consider yourself better than him, for you cannot tell how long you will remain in a state of grace. We are all frail; consider none more frail than yourself."[4]

9
PRAYER

Forgiveness involves letting go. Remember playing tug-of-war as a child? As long as the parties on each end of the rope are tugging, you have a "war." But when someone lets go, the war is over. When you forgive . . . , you are letting go of your end of the rope. . . . If you have released your end, the war is over for you.

—H. Norman Wright

The first time I experienced a panic attack, I felt like someone was slowly drawing the air out of my lungs, forcing me to fight to hold on to every breath. I remember it vividly: I was twenty-five, an immature young husband in the middle of a challenging seminary program, living off odd jobs, student loans, and generic macaroni and cheese. My life had all the makings of an emotional perfect storm.

What made matters worse was the fact that I had just completely given up on my faith. I was a pastor in training who didn't believe in God any longer. I didn't want to go to church on Christmas because I no longer accepted the virgin birth. My wife had to coerce me into going to church on Easter; I was convinced that the resurrection was a farce. I was mad at God and even angrier at the pace and fatigue of my everyday life. My world couldn't have been any more stressful than it already was—until I found out Lisa was pregnant.

She called me while I was at a conference in Chicago to tell me the news. Elated, I quickly went to the airport to fly home. While the plane was making its descent into Philadelphia International Airport, I felt my chest begin to anxiously tighten. Just seconds away from hearing the plane's tires hit the runway, with every seat full, flight attendants strapped in, all the passengers around me bracing themselves on their armrests for the landing, I ripped off my seatbelt, jumped out of my seat, and gasped for air. Everyone around me was startled, but none more than me, the guy from 23E who was looking around, clutching his chest and head, disoriented, and drenched in sweat. The flight attendant behind me yelled at me to sit down, which I did. Confused and scared, I began to take deep breaths until I slowly regained my composure. By the time we taxied into our gate at Terminal C, the mysterious feelings and sensations that ransacked my body were gone just as quickly as they came.

That plane ride kicked off one of the darkest, most excruciating periods of my life. For almost an entire year, I wrestled with the same question Steven Crane asked himself in his collection of poems *The Black Riders*:

> If I should cast off this tattered coat,
> And go free into the mighty sky;
> If I should find nothing there
> But a vast blue,

> Echoless, ignorant,—
>
> What then?[1]

Surely you've asked yourself that question. I've never known any-one who struggled with getting rid of the gorilla who hasn't asked himself, Is there really a God? and If so, why does he allow us to experience so much pain? I wrote my first book, *Second Guessing God*, to help people hang on while they struggle to find an answer to that question. Much of what I wrote in that book I learned in the first few years following my panicky plane flight. Suffice it to say that I've allowed myself to go free into the mighty sky, and what I discovered there is far from echoless and ignorant.

The panic attacks didn't last as long as my faith crisis, though. Learning about the toll stress and adrenaline take on the body helped quite a bit, as did beginning to exercise daily, getting a full night's sleep, and setting realistic expectations for the pace of my life. But by far the most important thing I did to help me get a handle on my panic attacks was memorize a number of key passages in the New Testament that promise relief from anxiety. Whenever I felt an attack coming on, I simply began to quote a Scripture verse to myself. Over time the Bible verses helped me pay attention to my body and my inner spiritual and emotional rhythms. Eventually, combined with the changes in my lifestyle, the perspective the Bible verses gave me proved too potent an antidote for my anxiety, and it simply faded away. I haven't had a panic attack since.

During that dark time, Philippians 4:6, 7 became my personal favorite passage: "Do not be anxious about anything, but in every-thing, by prayer and petition, with thanksgiving, present your requests to God. And the peace of God, which transcends all understanding, will guard your hearts and your minds in Christ Jesus."

Three things drew me to those verses.

First, they contain a command. "Do not be anxious" is an imperative (a command) in the original Greek. God won't allow us to let anxiety control us. Anxiety goes against God's best for our lives, and somehow knowing that God commanded me to stop being anxious gave me added resolve, on par with the feeling you get when a doctor orders you to stop doing something.

Second, the verses offer a remedy. Prayer is the cure for anxiety. In fact, the apostle Paul was so convinced that prayer is the solution to worry that to drive home his point he used three different Greek words: the words for *prayer* (*proseuche*), *supplication* (*deesis*), and *requests* (*aitemata*).[2] Scholars who debate the difference between each of these miss the point Paul is trying to make. Paul's intent seems to have been to grab every word available to him in the Greek language to underscore the fact that prayer escorts us into the presence of God and melts away whatever is worrying us.

Finally, these verses make a promise. Paul tells us that if we pray when we're anxious, the peace of God will guard our hearts and minds. The Greek word for *guard* is a military term used to describe the way a detachment of Roman soldiers would stand guard over a city to protect it from enemy assault.[3] During my dark time, whenever I felt an anxiety attack coming on, I pictured God himself physically standing in between me and the problem that was causing me to worry. Knowing that the all-powerful creator of the universe loves me so much that he would protect my heart and mind calmed me immensely.

Six or seven months after my first panic attack, my anxiety left, and I credited it all to the encouragement I found in Philippians 4:6, 7. I know that sounds very simplistic. Some people struggle with anxiety much longer than I did, even to the point of needing medication, but that's how it happened for me. As a result, that passage became one of my favorite verses in the Bible. It developed into a favorite text for my Bible studies and sermons and turned into a key passage for guiding other people when I had the opportunity to counsel them regarding worry. When people asked me to name the most important verses in the entire Bible, I always pointed to that passage. That passage saved me emotionally. You can understand, then, the awkwardness I felt years later when, upon fully studying the context of the book of Philippians, I discovered that the topic of anxiety isn't the focus of Philippians 4:6, 7 at all! The apostle Paul penned those words not so much because he wanted to tell us how to avoid panic attacks, but so we would know how to get rid of the gorilla.

One of the basic rules of biblical interpretation is to read whatever passage you are studying in context. Questions such as, What is the author's train of thought? and What precedes or follows this passage? should always be in the forefront of our minds to keep us from isolating a particular passage and making it say something it was not intended to say. Years later I discovered that in my rush to find help for my anxiety, I grabbed the wrong verses for all the right reasons. The core issue of Philippians 4:6, 7 isn't worry but how to deal with the toxic emotions we experience when we've been wounded and don't feel like backing down.

The verses immediately preceding Philippians 4:6, 7 help us understand the core issue Paul was addressing:

Therefore, my brothers, you whom I love and long for, my joy and crown, that is how you should stand firm in the Lord, dear friends!

I plead with Euodia and I plead with Syntyche to agree with each other in the Lord. Yes, and I ask you, loyal yokefellow, help these women who have contended at my side in the cause of the gospel, along with Clement and the rest of my fellow workers, whose names are in the book of life.

Rejoice in the Lord always. I will say it again: Rejoice! Let your gentleness be evident to all. The Lord is near (vv. 1-5).

Paul was not addressing anxiety specifically but the torrent of emotions caused by a knock-down, drag-out church fight between two women, Euodia and Syntyche. We don't know what the argument was about. We don't know the depth of the problem. We don't know who did what to whom. All we know is that the pain Euodia caused Syntyche or Syntyche caused Euodia was so severe that neither one was backing down anytime soon. In fact, their strained relationship was causing such church-wide heartache that the apostle Paul had to call on his close friends within the church ("loyal yokefellow") and church leaders like Clement to intervene.

But that's not all he did. In the midst of this intractable dispute, Paul directed Euodia and Syntyche and the other church leaders to prayer. Why? Because that's what disciples do: when followers of Christ find themselves overcome with anger toward someone who has hurt them, especially toward a fellow Christ follower, they go to their knees. Sometimes prayer is the only thing that can quiet an anxious, wounded heart.

PRAYER CALMS US DOWN

The Journal of John Woolman recounts a scene when Woolman, a Quaker who lived in colonial times in what is now New Jersey, tried to conduct a prayer meeting with a Native American tribe along the banks of the Susquehanna River in Pennsylvania. Woolman wrote, "On the evening of the 18th I was at their meeting, where pure gospel love was felt, to the tendering of some of our hearts. The interpreters endeavoured to acquaint the people of what I said in short sentences, but found some difficulty, as none of them were quite perfect in the English and Delaware tongues." Eventually Woolman decided to stop the interpreting and trust that God would work through his words alone and help those in attendance grasp the meaning of his prayers: "Afterward, feeling my mind covered with the spirit of prayer, I told the interpreters that I found it in my heart to pray to God, and believed, if I prayed right, He would hear me, and expressed my willingness for them to omit interpreting." After the meeting, Woolman learned that Papunehang, the Indian chief, approached one of the interpreters and said of the English prayer he had not understood, "I love to feel where words come from."[4]

I've always been struck by the innocent beauty of the chief's reaction, but it's pretty apparent to me that while Woolman was praying he wasn't simultaneously trying to get rid of the gorilla. If he had, the chief's reaction might have been a little different. I've read the prayers I've put into a journal years after a painful incident, and I've listened to the words coming out of the hearts of people struggling to find a way to forgive; there's nothing remotely endearing about any of them. For those of us who struggle with forgiveness, the place where words are formed is a place of constant agitation. It's the place where memories are replayed over and over again; where the original memories of a rapist's face or the words of an overbearing mother can't be easily forgotten. In my experience, feeling the place where the words of an unforgiving heart are formed is more like accidentally leaning on an electric fence than listening to someone recite a poem in a foreign language.

Years ago Lisa and I were traveling from Trenton, New Jersey, to the Jersey shore for the day. A white Volvo station wagon in front of us veered to the right, then turned hard left again and flipped over three times, coming to rest in the grass in the center median. In that split second I was more frightened than any other time I can remember. I quickly pulled over, and when Lisa and I jumped out, we were surprised to see small preschool-age children in the back seat. We reached in, grabbed one in each arm, and pulled them out. Lisa huddled with the children while I pried the driver- and passenger-side doors open and helped a man and woman, both covered in blood, slide out of their seats. Since these were the days before cell phones, I ran out into the freeway, stopped a car, and asked someone to go get help. Twenty minutes later an ambulance showed up and took them all to the hospital.

I'll never forget what I saw in that car, but more important, I'll never forget what I felt—a knot in my chest and a mad rush of adrenaline covered by a blanket of numbness. It's the only situation that's ever come close to mirroring the immediate emotional aftereffects of getting ransacked by the gorilla. The place where unforgiving words are formed is a dark, erratic, and anxious place.

When the gorilla moves in, the first thing he unpacks is anxiety. Anxiety masks the real issues involved in forgiving those who have hurt us by locking us into replaying what happened to us over and over and over again. Rather than giving us ways to move on from the pain we've experienced, anxiety keeps us trapped in a nonstop mental replay of how we were hurt, complete with all the bewildering emotions we felt when the hurt first happened. Anxiety makes our situation seem more painful and intractable than it actually is, if for no other reason than the more we replay the memories, the more ingrained they become.

As disciples our best weapon against anxiety is prayer. Prayer opens up the windows in our souls and allows fresh air to whip around the corridors of our past, opening up the possibility for new ways of looking at what we have experienced.

MY MONTHLY TRIP TO THE MONASTERY

Years ago I began the practice of going to a monastery once a month to devote myself to prayer for an entire day. Through the years I discovered that while my daily morning time for prayer is essential for my personal growth, if I really wanted to hear from God I needed to get away and completely detach myself from my usual routine. This became even more essential about ten years ago when I became serious about extracting the gorilla's paws from every area of my life. As I've discussed in previous chapters, it's important for us to remember that forgiveness is first and foremost a spiritual problem, and if we are having trouble forgiving someone that might be just as much a commentary on our ability to connect with God as it is on anything else. Once I began to realize this, it became apparent that I couldn't just skim the surface of my soul any longer. I needed to dig deep, so I began heading off to monasteries to pay attention to my inner life long enough for God to really speak to me. Luke 5:16 tells us that "Jesus often withdrew to lonely places and prayed." If you're serious about getting rid of the gorilla, I'd like to encourage you to do the same.

Here's a quick sketch of what I've been doing once a month now for almost twelve years:

7:00 AM. I arrive at a local monastery and try to avoid the eighty-year-old nuns who ask me if I have lunch plans (for some reason elderly nuns think I'm hot). For fifteen or twenty dollars for the day, most places give me lunch and a small hotel-like room, with a bed, table, and lamp. You can find places like this around where you live by searching online for "Catholic retreat centers."

7:00–9:00 AM. I pull out a yellow pad of paper and do a "data dump." I write down everything that is swirling around in my brain: things stressing me, to-do lists, things I'm putting off, persistent sins, people I need to forgive, books I want to read. I write down anything and everything about my family, my work, my finances. The goal is to clear everything out of my mind and put it on paper. I keep that tablet with me the rest of the day. If any other idea or question or sin pops into my mind throughout the day, I quickly write it down and let the tablet "hold" the stress or weight of it.

9:00–10:30 AM. I'm exhausted. I go for a long hike in the woods behind the monastery. I try really hard not to talk to God during this time, just listen. Most of the time I watch deer, skip rocks in the creek, or throw another idea that pops into my head onto that tablet. Sometimes I'll flip my Bible open to a passage that comes to mind.

10:30 AM–noon. I meditate on one small passage of Scripture. Sometimes something will hit me, and I'll spend the rest of the day studying that passage. Other times I'll yawn and start playing "Bible Roulette." Some of my greatest spiritual insights have come during this hour-and-a-half period of time.

Noon–1:00 PM. I eat. Monasteries are known for plain but plentiful food. I usually sit with a nun or two and ask them about their lives. They're usually more interested in serving me than in finding out what I do and why I'm there. Marianist sisters are wonderful. So are Sisters of the Precious Blood.

If I'm really struggling to forgive someone or working through a serious sin that has me entangled, I'll skip lunch and fast. Abba John the Short, one of the Desert Fathers, said, "If a king wants to take a city whose citizens are hostile, he first captures the food and water of the inhabitants of the city, and when they are starving subdues them. . . . If a man is earnest in fasting and hunger, the enemies which trouble his soul will grow weak."[5]

1:00–2:30 PM. I take a nap in my room.

2:30–4:30 PM. Here's the point during my day when, if God is going to speak to me in a profound way, it happens. By this point in the day, my mind is clear and my heart is still. I take out a pad of paper and write down three words: *sins*, *strengths*, and *schedule*. I ask God to be brutally honest with me regarding what sins need to be eradicated from my life, what areas of strength I need to focus on, and where my schedule needs to change.

4:30–5:00 PM. I take all my scribbling for the day and condense it onto a one-page piece of paper and tuck it into my Bible. All my other pieces of paper get trashed.

5:00 PM. I walk through the monastery chapel one last time and take a long, deep breath. I stand there, drink in one last moment of the place, and then duck my head out the door and head for home.

EVERYONE'S GORILLA

Here's one of the serious, rarely discussed side effects of an unforgiving heart that justifies going away to a monastery once a month to try to eradicate it: when we wrestle with the gorilla, everyone in our life wrestles with him too. The effects of an unforgiving heart can't be contained in one nice little area of our lives. The gorilla can't be isolated. We can't keep him locked up somewhere. The gorilla affects everyone and everything around us. The place I've seen this most is in my marriage.

I've always had two distinct challenges in my relationship with my wife. The first has always been the fact that I'm not real relationally intuitive. For instance, I'm horrible at buying gifts for Lisa. For her first birthday after we were married, one of the gifts I bought her was James Dobson's book *What Wives Wish Their Husbands Knew About Women*. As soon as she opened it, a funny grin immediately crossed her face.

"What?" I asked.

"I really appreciate the gift, but aren't wives supposed to give these to their husbands?" she replied.

Awkward pause.

"Maybe I felt that you needed to know all the things that I needed to know about you as a wife. Did you ever think about that?" I said.

That gift sort of set the pace for the next twenty years.

A few years later, Lisa had said that she wanted something practical for her birthday, so I got her a cordless phone. When she opened it up, she held it in the air and said, "Hey, how 'bout this? A phone!"

"You said something practical! We needed a cordless phone, so I got you a phone."

"It's nice and everything, but I was hoping for something a little more personal and heartfelt than a household item."

Taking that advice to heart, the next year for our anniversary I got her a vacuum cleaner, which was a step up from the time I got her sneakers. Finally, a few years ago I put cash in a birthday card along with a little note that read, "I give up. I think this is what you want." When she opened the card, looked over at me and slowly raised one eyebrow, I knew I was headed straight for the Dr. Phil show.

The gift that took the cake was, ironically, the one I felt was just supergenius on my part. I paid attention all year to what Lisa said she really needed, and all I heard was how she couldn't lose those few extra pounds of pregnancy weight. I talked to all my guy friends, and we all agreed I should get her a treadmill. Listen to me. If you are a man and you can take away only one thing from this book, let it be this: never ask your guy friends what they think your wife would like for her birthday. Ask *her* friends. Ask Jesus. Ask anyone but your fishing buddies.

My other difficulty, besides being romantically challenged, is that I'm stubborn. You can back me into a corner in an argument and if I think I'm right, even if there's a slight chance I'm not, I won't back down. God has worked on me over the years, but I still have a long way to go. For instance, what I didn't tell you about that conference I attended in Chicago while I was in seminary was that the day before I left I shot a hole in my couch.

Gangs from Trenton had been coming into our apartment complex and stealing cars, and knowing that I would be gone an entire week, Lisa was understandably nervous. To allay her fears, I pulled my deer-hunting 20-gauge pump shotgun out of the bedroom closet and showed her how to load bullets, called deer slugs, into the gun. Once the shells were in the gun, I pointed it to the ceiling and said, "If you hear someone outside trying to get in, simply put these shells in the gun and shoot at the top of the door. I guarantee that will make them run." I gave Lisa a ten-minute lecture on the ins and outs of gun safety, and then I slowly took the shells out of the gun and began carefully placing them back into the case.

"There's still a bullet in the gun," Lisa said.

"No there's not."

"Yes there is. You put five in there."

"Sorry. I've been doing this way longer than you have. There were only four."

"No there weren't!"

"Yes there were!"

Frustrated that Lisa would question my judgment, I took the gun out again. Aiming at the couch, I said, "Listen. Even if there was a bullet in here, which there isn't, and it went off, it wouldn't hurt anything because of the concrete wall of our bedroom. But just to prove my point, watch this. I'm aiming at the couch. If there was a shell in the chamber, when I pulled this trigger you would hear—" *BOOM!* The shotgun kicked back and hit my shoulder and smoke instantly filled the room.

Finally Lisa broke the awkward silence. "Hey, Mr. Gun Safety, you just killed our couch!" I ran over and saw a huge hole in the couch's pillow, another massive hole in the back of the couch itself, and an even larger hole behind it in the drywall. Running into the bedroom, I saw that the shell had gone through the family room wall and into our bed! I was beside myself. The neighbors came outside and started walking around the apartment complex, wondering what happened. The whole time Lisa paced back and forth in the kitchen. "Maybe the neighbors will think a dresser fell on the floor or something," I said sheepishly. Her stare told me she didn't think I was too clever.

It was quite a scene. In fact, Lisa was so freaked out by what happened that she refused to sleep in the bed that night, afraid the shell would explode. I told her that's not how deer slugs work, but by that time I had already proven that my firearms expertise left much to be desired. The next day I did what I knew I had to do—I gave away all of my guns, and I haven't hunted since. In my mind there are some things in life you get a second chance with. Guns aren't one of them. Fortunately for me, marriage is.

Every so often, my relational clumsiness will get Lisa and me into a minor marital spat that my pride and stubbornness escalates into a two- or three-day dispute. It's embarrassing, really. Part of the blame lies with my fundamental immaturity. Part of it lies with my temperament. Mostly, however, my penchant for shooting myself in the marital foot comes from my inability to keep the gorilla locked in one room of my life. Those of us who wrestle with unforgiving hearts can't channel our rage, distance, and pessimism with laser-like precision toward only the people who originally hurt us. Like a swollen dam, our finely honed coping mechanisms spill over into every relationship we have.

Eventually, whether we like it or not, our gorilla becomes everyone's gorilla. The people we love most in this world begin getting hurt by us and as a result start hurting us in return. Instead of the gorilla affecting only my relationship with the person who originally hurt me way back when, he starts screwing up every relationship I have. Pretty soon I start seeing faces all over the place that I need to forgive. More important, people start viewing me as someone who needs to be forgiven rather than someone who needs to forgive. What once was a dispute between two parties has become an ever-expanding circle of conflict.

The painful secret held by everyone who lives with the gorilla is that we have just as much difficulty forgiving ourselves for the pain we've caused other people as we do forgiving those who originally caused us pain. As I'll talk about in the following chapter, the person I need to forgive most in this world is the person staring back at me in the mirror. I feel immense hatred toward those who have hurt me in the past, but I feel even more antipathy toward myself for allowing what those people did to me to change me into something I never wanted to become.

When I find myself in a stalemate with my wife, the sweetest, most kindhearted person I know, it is usually because I took something she said the wrong way and then responded unkindly. Her response makes me even angrier, which in turn pushes her away even more. My temperament, my overreactions, everything about my childish demeanor, all causes her to become something she never wanted to become either. Each of us shares words we wish we could take back. Each of us becomes embarrassed over the way we reacted. Each of us begins to look an awful lot like Euodia or Syntyche.

When we're locked in this childlike battle of the will, unwilling to back down, both deeply wounded, we realize that if not for a power outside of our relationship, we might be in for a really tough road. The anxiety we feel, the tenseness in our chests, the rush of adrenaline—it all begins to feel like an unassailable barricade. Fortunately, something always prods us to get away from the situation—to the mall, to a state park, to a monastery, to the car—so we can still our hearts and engage in the only thing that can move us beyond this impasse: prayer. After a brief time away to connect with God and allow his thoughts to fill our minds and his peace to fill our hearts, we'll come back to each other, souls still, minds clear, able to have an honest, constructive discussion about how we can change, forgive, and move on.

I can't help but think about you right now. Who is the person you just can't bring yourself to talk to? Who came to your mind as you were reading this chapter? Is it someone in your church? Your spouse? Your ex? A pastor? A formerly close friend? A sibling? Your mother? I wonder if one of the reasons God had us cross paths was so I could share this thought with you now: if you're having trouble forgiving someone who's hurt you, then maybe God wants you to stop trying. Maybe you're not ready yet. Instead, maybe all he's expecting you to do right now is to get away from the situation and commit yourself to prayer.

Sometimes prayer is the only thing that can quiet an anxious, wounded heart.

Maybe that's enough for right now.

IO

MIRROR

For some are too proud to forgive themselves, till the forgiveness of God has had its way with them, has drowned their pride in the tears of repentance, and made their heart come again like the heart of a little child.

—George MacDonald

One of these days I'm going to publish a book called *Notes to My Daughters*, a manuscript with an intended audience of only three people. Over the years I've tried, with some regularity, to record funny stories, sayings, observations, and musings about my three daughters as they've grown up before my eyes. My goal has been to record the precious snapshots of their lives before they irretrievably disappear into the past. I figure I'll give my daughters the book when the youngest graduates from college. My guess is that my grandkids will get more of a kick out of it than anyone.

I'm titling one section of the book "Funny Stories." In Camryn's part (Camryn is my youngest and probably most strong willed), I'll share the story about how I devised a genius parenting technique—one that I am sure will soon be shared in parenting seminars for years to come—when she was close to hitting the "terrible twos." One day she was in the middle of a typical twenty-month-old's tantrum—she was tired, frantic, minutes away from naptime, rolling around in her bed screaming for a juice cup that I'd hand to her and she'd throw right back on the floor. As I watched this, I stood there playing with my belly button (don't ask me why—parents of two-year-olds do strange things!). Then, for some reason I lifted my finger to my nose and smelled it. The stench was horrible!

A parental light bulb went off. I picked the cup off the floor again and put my index finger, the one I had put in my smelly belly button, on top of the lid. Leaning over the bed, I placed the cup's lid and my index finger close to Camryn's nose and said, "Honey, you don't want that cup. It's stinky. See?" Seconds later a puzzled expression came across her face as she squinted and said, "Tinky. It tinky, Daddy." Not wanting the cup any longer, she rolled over and immediately fell asleep. Shocked, I slowly tip-toed out of her room, shut the door behind me, held my arms in the air, fingers pointing back at me, and whispered, "Who's the parenting genius? I'm the parenting genius!" From then on, whenever I found myself facing an irrational obsession with a toy or something else, I'd use the "It's stinky" technique, and it worked like a charm. I know I'm going to hell, but it worked every time.

In my book I'll include other stories too, like the time I found Chandler, not quite two years of age, covered from head to toe in permanent marker. Lisa and I were one hour away from taking the girls to a Christmas party, pretty frilly dresses and all, and somehow Kelsey managed to find a box full of permanent markers. Unbeknownst to us, she got Chandler to take off all of her clothes in the bathroom and then proceeded to decorate Chandler's entire body—huge circles around her eyes, nose, and lips; dozens of lines up and down her arms and legs; ears filled in with red ink; lines in the scalp of her light blonde hair; even circles around her little boobies—all with permanent markers! I was in the other room when I heard Lisa scream, "Oh my gosh!" and I ran to find out what was the matter. I just stood there and laughed; Lisa, because we were just minutes away from needing to leave, didn't think the situation was quite as humorous! I still can picture her leaning over the bathtub scrubbing every mark off Chandler's tiny body.

Kelsey, because she is the oldest, has a few more stories in the book so far. One of the more recent ones is about the time in sixth grade when a boy asked her to go to the movies, an invitation to which I responded, as any good Christian father would, "When you turn thirty." Somehow she persuaded us to allow her to go if (A) she went with a group of friends, (B) her sisters tagged along, and (C) Lisa and I went to a movie in the adjacent theater. As she walked into the theater, Kelsey told me that the boy, who was just as sweet as could be, had a peanut allergy. When I heard that, I disappeared for a few minutes and then reappeared with a bag full of roasted nuts from the snack counter. As I tried to rub them on Kelsey's lips, she pulled back and said, "Eeew, Dad, don't. He's allergic." To which I replied, "Precisely."

Notes to My Daughters will be packed with funny stories, but that's not all. I want to capture the tender moments, the hard questions the girls asked, the tears, the laughter, and the great times we've had on family vacations. There's also a section I'm tempted to leave out, but I know if I'm to provide a balanced, realistic portrait of their childhoods, I must include it. It's a section entitled "I'm Sorry." This is the part of the book where I'll apologize for all the things I did while the girls were growing up that, because they were so young, they didn't understand the full effects of on their lives.

I'll apologize for the fact that while I was in seminary and the first few years of the pastorate, I didn't make enough money for Lisa to stay at home full-time. I'll never forget the day Lisa walked out the door in tears to go back to work after her three-month maternity leave. I'll apologize for the time a few years back when Lisa was gone for a couple of days and I had the girls all by myself. I was stressed, thoroughly consumed by some major problems at our church, and the girls were fighting with one another and unwilling to help out at the dinner table. As I put lukewarm fish sticks and macaroni and cheese on the table someone complained, and I completely flipped out by slamming my palm down on the table and swearing. All three girls sat in shock. Never before (and not since) had they seen me act and talk like that.

I'll apologize for the skipped pages at bedtime. I'll apologize for the deep, heart-wrenching conversations that I occasionally passed off to their mother. I'll apologize for not making the time to drive them over to see their grandparents more. I'll apologize for lots of things I just can't seem to forgive myself for. In the end, I'm not quite sure if that part of the book will be more for them, or for me.

The hardest person for me to forgive has always been the one staring back at me in the mirror. Things I've said play over and over again in my head like a CD stuck on repeat, the faces of people I've hurt stuck in my memory like a video that's been paused. The emotions, the twinge of guilt in my gut, the pain in their faces—I relive it over and over again. I can talk all I want about how people have hurt me in the past, but the reality is I've hurt just as many people as people have hurt me.

My hunch is that because you've had such a hard time getting rid of the gorilla, forgiving yourself might be one of your struggles too.

Maybe you had an abortion when you were younger.

Maybe you went through a rebellious period in your life.

Maybe you physically hurt someone in some way.

Maybe you found yourself wrapped up in an affair.

Maybe you were in the military and can't forget the things you saw and did.

Maybe you were involved in an accident that seriously injured someone.

Maybe you made some bad decisions in a difficult relationship that left hurting people in your wake.

If so, here's something you must understand: you can't authentically extend forgiveness to anyone until you've first extended it to yourself. Being able to forgive means you understand grace and why it should be offered. If you can't show grace to yourself, every time you tell people you forgive them your words are marked by sincerity and hollowness at the same time—sincerity because you want to forgive, but hollowness because your gestures of forgiveness come from a garden whose fruit you have not allowed yourself to eat. As a result, every word of forgiveness smacks of hypocrisy, not to your recipient's ears, but to your own. You may mouth all the correct words and exhibit the appropriate overtures of forgiveness, but your heart is not in them. To truly get rid of the gorilla, you must be able to forgive yourself. Let me share a few things I've learned that might help you in this difficult task.

TWO KINDS OF GUILT

The first thing that helped me reach a point where I was finally able to forgive myself was understanding the difference between God-inspired guilt and phantom guilt.

GOD-INSPIRED GUILT

God-inspired guilt stems from something you *should* feel guilty about. Contrary to what some teach today, there are things you should feel guilty about doing, horribly guilty in fact. God's Word provides a clear description of how we should live our lives and how we shouldn't. When we fail to follow God's plan for our lives, the Bible calls that behavior sin, and when we sin against God, other people, and ourselves, God himself, in the form of the Holy Spirit, begins to work in our hearts to cause us to feel remorse for what we have done. Speaking of the Holy Spirit in John 16:8, Jesus said, "When he comes, he will convict the world of guilt in regard to sin and righteousness and judgment." That feeling of conviction is intended to lead us to ask God for forgiveness, and when we do that, the Bible promises we can be 100 percent assured that God has forgiven us, completely and without reservation (1 John 1:8, 9). Our sin is irretrievably removed "as far as the east is from the west" (Psalm 103:12), never to be brought up by God again.

The hope is that the person we hurt would forgive us as well, but even if he or she declines our request for forgiveness, that does not negate the fact that we stand before God completely and thoroughly forgiven. As a result, God's use of conviction to produce guilt has served its purpose—to lead us to withdraw from harmful behaviors and to seek forgiveness. Once that happens, our God-inspired guilt subsides. It doesn't surface again until a different behavior arises that God wants us to stop.

For example, when I first went to college to train to become a pastor, I did an internship at a church in Lancaster, Ohio. Because the pastor of this church was a loving man and an outstanding communicator, I had high hopes for what would occur that summer. I was extremely disappointed when the church's many problems kept preventing the pastor from spending much time with me. His love for his people and his willingness to sacrifice on their behalf reminded me of the pastor in Chaucer's *Canterbury Tales*:

> His parish was wide and its houses far apart,
> but he never neglected—for rain or thunder,
> sickness or trouble—to visit on foot,
> with a staff in his hand,
> the furthest in his parish, great or humble.
> He gave this noble example to his sheep:
> that he practiced first and preached afterwards.[1]

The pastor was so busy he rarely had time to spend with me, and I was angry. I became very critical of him behind his back to other people in the church.

Near the end of my internship, we attended a conference together, and during one of the worship services at the conference we sat next to one another. While we sang, I felt an immense sense of guilt over the way I had been treating him. Here I was worshiping

God while standing next to a Christian brother I had been bitterly slandering.

Consumed with God-inspired guilt, I leaned over and said, "I have something to confess to you" and shared everything I had been saying about him and why. To my surprise he reached out and hugged me and told me he was sorry for not spending time with me and that he completely forgave me for what I had done. It was a spiritual moment I will never forget. That's what God-inspired guilt does—it leads us to repentance and hopefully to reconciliation. God-inspired guilt is a beautiful thing.

PHANTOM GUILT

Phantom guilt, on the other hand, is an ugly thing that consumes our minds and saps our spiritual strength. Phantom guilt is lingering guilt for something you should no longer feel guilty about.

In his classic Christian book *The Pilgrim's Progress*, John Bunyan tells the parable of a man named Christian who has been making his way back to the celestial city with a massive burden tied to his back. The load has become excruciatingly painful to carry, and as the parable continues it becomes apparent that the load represents the weight of Christian's past sins. Eventually Christian comes to the foot of the cross, and as Bunyan puts it: "His burden loosed from off his shoulders, and fell from off his back, and began to tumble; and so continued to do till it came to the mouth of the sepulchre, where it fell in, and I saw it no more."[2]

Phantom guilt is what happens when we go back to that sepulcher, dig up that large tote full of our past sins, and reaffix it onto our backs. Phantom guilt is feeling guilty over something that has already been forgiven. The primary reason we feel phantom guilt is because of how our brains and emotions work. When I do something that goes against God's plan, my brain records that incident with amazing clarity, and once I am forgiven, God doesn't go inside my head and delete that memory. As a result, I confuse myself into thinking that just because I can remember that incident, God automatically remembers it as well.

What makes matters worse is that our brains trigger certain emotions when those memories are recalled, so we remember not only the sins we've committed but the emotions of God-inspired guilt we felt afterward as well. Those memories and feelings of guilt are phantoms. They exist inside our minds, so they feel real, but they don't exist in the mind of God. Once we asked for forgiveness, God forgave and completely forgot what we did. It's gone. In his mind it no longer exists. The problem is it is still very real to us.

The solution, then, is to remind ourselves as soon as phantom guilt rears its ugly head that what we are experiencing is not real; it is a shadow of something that used to exist. We have to discipline ourselves to trust the fact of our forgiveness over the feelings of our phantom guilt.

Over the years I've told the story in my sermons about the time my family and I were eating at a restaurant and out of the corner of my eye I saw a baby sitting in a high chair near her mother. My jaw dropped and my eyes started to mist, and I stood up and walked across the room to where the baby and her mother sat. I looked at the young woman and just smiled. She stared at me and smiled in return.

"She's beautiful," I said. "What's her name?"

"Jessica."

"I'm proud of you."

"Thanks."

Then I just stood there for a moment, grinning at both of them.

When I went back to our table, Lisa asked, "What was that all about?"

"A year and a half ago, someone dragged that young woman sitting over there, kicking and screaming, into my office to talk. She was seventeen, pregnant, and scared to death. Her boyfriend left her when he found out she was expecting. Her parents were in the process of kicking her out of the house. The day I talked with her, she had decided she was going to have an abortion. I tried my best to talk her out of it and connected her with people who could help, but I never heard what happened afterward. That's her baby over there."

Every time I tell that story in a sermon, I can count on two or three women, usually in their mid thirties, coming up and asking to talk after the service. Usually the first words out of their mouths are all the same: "I wish you wouldn't tell stories like that. I think about what I did every single day of my life." I gently talk to them about God's grace and how he wants them to move on. Usually they tell me that they understand all of that, but they still can't find the strength to forgive themselves for what they've done. At some point I end up telling them what I want to tell you right now: There comes a time when you've beaten yourself up enough to last two or three lifetimes. God wants you to feel OK about moving on and feeling good about yourself and your life again. Either the cross was good enough to pay for everyone's sins, including yours, or it wasn't. This guilt you are feeling is a phantom. It's not coming from God, and it's not going to undo the past. Let it go. It's OK. God really wants you to move on.

AT THE ALTAR OF PHANTOM GUILT

It's hard to overexaggerate how much God hates idols. The very first commandment of the Ten Commandments strictly forbids idols of any kind: "You shall have no other gods before me. You shall not make for yourself an idol in the form of anything in heaven above or on the earth beneath or in the waters below" (Exodus 20:3, 4).

We don't think much about idols today, but in the Old Testament God's people really struggled with idol worship. Mainly farmers, they lived and died by the amount of rainfall they received each year. Oftentimes they would get hit with a scorching drought and risk losing an entire year's worth of crops. Faced with the possibility of being unable to feed their families when those times hit, they had a tendency to quickly begin praying to anything they thought could help, including the gods of the Canaanite people who lived in their midst. The Canaanites didn't believe in one God; they believed in multiple gods, and the one that tended to be the biggest thorn in Israel's side was Baal—the god of storms, springs, and water. He is always pictured on ancient clay tablets with a thunderbolt in his hand.

God hated idol worship then (and hates it now) for reasons that are obvious: He alone wanted Israel's affection, trust, and worship. Idols disrupt a person's relationship with God so deeply that God sent prophet after prophet to communicate how much he hated their influence in his people's lives. As if mocking the fact that his people spent so much time with pagan idols they had forgotten who he was, God said through the prophet Isaiah, "I am the LORD; that is my name! I will not give my glory to another or my praise to idols" (Isaiah 42:8). Jonah cried out in the pit of the whale, "Those who cling to worthless idols forfeit the grace that could be theirs" (Jonah 2:8). Tearing down the "high places" on top of hills and mountains where pagan idols were worshiped constantly ran high on God's to-do list for an Old Testament king. Sadly, the worship of idols led in part to the overthrow of southern Israel by the Babylonian empire and the loss of thousands of lives (Jeremiah 7). Idol worship is serious stuff in the eyes of God.

It comes as no surprise, then, that the early church picked up God's abhorrence of idol worship and warned new Christians to avoid its dangers. "Flee from idolatry" the apostle Paul wrote to the church in Corinth (1 Corinthians 10:14). "Dear children, keep yourselves from idols" wrote the apostle John (1 John 5:21). The apostle Peter seemed to pick up the prophet Isaiah's mantle when he warned the early Christians, "You have spent enough time in the past doing what pagans choose to do—living in debauchery, lust, drunkenness, orgies, carousing and detestable idolatry" (1 Peter 4:3).

One interesting twist we find in the New Testament is that the biblical writers were led by the Holy Spirit to broaden the definition of idolatry. Colossians 3:5 says, "Put to death, therefore, whatever belongs to your earthly nature: sexual immorality, impurity, lust, evil desires and greed, which is idolatry." Lust and greed are not actual physical idols, but the result of engaging in those activities is the same as idol worship—it disrupts a person's relationship with God. Lust and greed, in effect, become idolatrous activities. Under this broader definition, an idol is anything that diverts our attention and trust away from God himself. With that in mind, it's easy for those of us who struggle with forgiving ourselves to see how our phantom guilt has become our own personal idol.

Phantom guilt is consuming. It's like a bad tooth that you can't get pulled—it's always with you and you think about it constantly. The smallest, most unrelated things seem to trigger memories from the past, and we end up asking God for forgiveness over and over and over again. Something triggers a memory, we feel another rush of guilt, and that prompts us to go back to God for his mercy all over again. The whole time God looks at us and says, "I've already forgiven you for this." But that doesn't matter to us; we just keep going back. We become consumed with phantom guilt rather than consumed with God; phantom guilt becomes an idol whose altar we just can't leave.

The problem is God hated idol worship in the Old Testament, he hated it in the New Testament, and we can be sure he hates it now. Idol worship is something that God absolutely will not tolerate and must be discontinued immediately. If you can't forgive yourself because of God's grace, maybe you can forgive yourself out of respect for how much God hates the worship of idols.

ANOTHER LESSON FROM THE LORD'S PRAYER

The prayer that Jesus taught his disciples to pray in Matthew 6:9-13, typically called the Lord's Prayer, illustrates my point. Notice two things about the following verses:

This, then, is how you should pray:

"Our Father in heaven,
hallowed be your name,
your kingdom come,
your will be done
   on earth as it is in heaven.
Give us today our daily bread.
Forgive us our debts,
   as we also have forgiven our debtors.
And lead us not into temptation,
but deliver us from the evil one.

First, Jesus said, "This, then, is how you should pray," not "This, then, is *what* you should pray." I've always thought it odd that certain religious groups encourage their people to pray the Lord's Prayer over and over again. They miss the point. The prayer, also called the model prayer, is an outline of what to pray *about*, not actual words to be prayed. It's like a cheat sheet to give structure to our prayer time so we pray for the right things in the right progression.

Second, notice there are six kinds of things Jesus tells us to include in prayer. Here they are in order:

Hallowed be your name.

Your kingdom come.

Your will be done.

Give us today our daily bread.

Forgive us our debts.

Lead us not into temptation.

These six petitions tell us the subjects that we are to give attention to as we pray. We should start out a time of prayer by worshiping and honoring God; then we should focus our minds on the expansion of his rule in our lives. Next we should move on to asking him to align our desires with his will. Next we should turn our attention to praying for specific things we need in life, and then we should ask for forgiveness for personal sins. Finally, the prayer outline concludes with a request for personal protection from the evil one.

Here's my question: which petition is the request for personal forgiveness? Is it first, second, or even third? No, it's not even fourth. It's fifth! Personal forgiveness of sins against God, others, and ourselves ranks fifth in an outline of six things Jesus asks us to focus on in prayer. I don't know about you, but I'm impressed by this.

Until I was able to forgive myself, here's how my prayers usually started:

Dear God, please forgive me for _____.

Dear God, I'm so sorry that_____.

Dear God, I'm unworthy to talk to you today because _____
_____.

What did all these prayers have in common? ME. They all started with me! It didn't matter that I was trying to deal with my sins; my prayers always began in a self-centered fashion. But what Jesus seems to be teaching us through the model prayer is that the most important thing we can do to get rid of the gorilla is to put our sins and guilt into proper perspective. The worship of God is paramount. Nothing should come in the way of that. Next is the expansion of his kingdom rule in our lives and our willingness to accept his will, regardless. Beyond that, high on God's list of priorities is making sure we have what we need for the day. All of these rank higher in priority than simply rattling off a laundry list of personal sins we've committed since the last time we prayed.

Jesus' message couldn't be clearer: "Lighten up and stop beating yourself up! Cut yourself some slack! I know you sin. You know you sin. There will never be a time when you won't sin. I say this not to encourage you to sin, but to give you some perspective. There are more important things to be consumed with than your personal shortcomings."

Oswald Chambers said it this way, "Am I willing to reduce myself simply to 'me,' determinedly to strip myself of all my friends think of me, of all I think of myself, and to hand that simple naked self over to God?"[3] That's the real issue. Can we simply *be*? Can we simply allow ourselves to be, to exist, to sit, to rest in the presence of God, content to bask in the sufficiency of his grace and allowing him to take his rightful place as the focal point of our lives?

Or will we create idols out of our phantom guilt?

The philosopher Blaise Pascal is known for what has been called "Pascal's Wager," the idea that when a person decides not to become a Christian he is taking an immense gamble: If it turns out that there isn't a God, then when he dies, he's won the gamble. If it turns out there is a God, and also a real place called hell, and he's chosen to do nothing about it, then he's lost the wager.

After Pascal's death, someone discovered a scrap of paper sewn inside the lining of his coat. Evidently Pascal had been carrying that small piece of paper around for eight years. On the paper were scribbled the following words:

The year of Grace, 1654

Monday, 23 November, feast of Saint Clement, Pope
and Martyr, and of others in the Martyrology.

Eve of Saint Chrysogonus, Martyr and others.

From about half past ten in the evening until half
past midnight.

Fire

'God of Abraham, God of Isaac, God of Jacob,' not
of philosophers and scholars.

Certainty, certainty, heartfelt, joy, peace.[4]

No one is quite sure what experience Pascal is referring to, but
that's the closest description I've ever read of the way I felt the first
time I realized that God's grace was meant for me too. It was like a
flame, a burning in my heart. I was overcome with a sense of light-
ness and energy. I felt free to believe that God wasn't out to pay me
back for my past sins. I felt it was OK to move on and not just to work
for God's best in my life but to begin to expect it. For two straight
hours Pascal felt this feeling. That's a shame—because I'm not sure
that feeling is meant to ever go away. There's nothing quite like the
feeling of finally realizing that God's grace is meant for everyone on
the planet, including you and me.

OUR MISTAKES FOR HIS GLORY

The final thing that helped me come to the point where I could forgive myself was realizing that God could use even my past mistakes
to accomplish his purposes in the lives of those whom I've hurt. In

God's economy nothing is ever wasted, including pain. Romans 8:28 reminds us that "in all things God works for the good of those who love him." In all things—that includes the bad stuff we experience as well as the good. That includes the bad stuff we do to other people, not just the bad stuff they do to us. This doesn't make light of or condone the things we've done; it's simply acknowledging that God can take the most hateful thing we've ever done and turn it around to accomplish his will and purpose in someone else's life.

While finishing graduate school, I worked each summer in the maintenance department of a large financial services company, helping to care for its landscaping and beautiful rolling lawn. Early on I could tell that the guys on the maintenance crew weren't real thrilled with having a pastor in training on their team, but their misgivings only strengthened my resolve to reach out to them and convert them to Christ. My first week on the job, I adopted the guys on my crew as my spiritual project. I remember praying, "Jesus, when I leave this place, I want every person on my team to be a Christian."

At that place in my spiritual journey, I had already proved myself to be a fervent evangelist, so I assumed my goal would be easily attained. The first part of my strategy was to set myself apart by living a noticeably moral life. I worked harder and longer than anybody on my team. I refused to join in when the guys told dirty jokes and swore, and whenever we were in the locker room I made sure never to look at the pictures of naked women hanging on the walls. The second part of my strategy was to insert spiritual ideas into our conversations, to provoke discussions about God and faith. Some would have called this picking a fight, but at the time I called it witnessing.

I zeroed in almost immediately on one man named Andrew. In his early forties, Andrew had just moved to the states from Poland with his family. He could barely speak English, so most of our conversations revolved around Andrew pointing to things and asking, "Brian, what English word for . . . ?" I figured Andrew would be the easiest on our team to reach, so I chose every assignment I could get that involved working with him. I discovered that Andrew was a former Catholic and had little interest in spiritual matters; however, this didn't deter me in the least. With the zeal of a pushy door-to-door salesman, I forced spiritual matters into just about every conversation Andrew and I had.

Near the end of the summer, I was talking with Andrew and casually posed a question to him: "Andrew, we're friends, right?"

He took me by surprise when he answered no.

Shocked, I asked, "What do you mean? We've been working together an entire summer."

He answered, "Brian, what you call people . . . you know . . . you talk with them . . . you work with them . . . they are nice people . . . you go home and don't see them until you go to work again?"

"Acquaintances?"

"Yes, acquaintances. I have many acquaintances. In Poland, our word for *friend* is special. In Poland, when we call a person *friend*, it means that we share hearts with that person. So, to answer your question: in America, I do not have any friends yet."

Before I knew it, the summer came to a close and I returned to school full-time, but when I came back to the maintenance crew the following year I was a different person. I had spent most of the intervening months at school sorting out an excruciating crisis of faith that I described in the previous chapter. I started my first day on the job thoroughly broken. I was still a believer, but I felt as if I had just come out of surgery with a bandaged soul. More important, during that crisis of faith I had an opportunity to evaluate the kind of Christ follower I was becoming. I realized that I had been a real jerk, especially around Andrew. When I came to this realization, I became convinced that any hope of reaching Andrew for Christ had been irrevocably lost. Instead of being a witness for Christ, I had been an idiot for Christ.

Gone were the spiritual bravado and pushiness from the summer before, replaced by a few things that were new to me: empathy, respect, and patience. I think Andrew was puzzled by the change in me, because late one afternoon he asked if I still believed in God. I looked at the ground and slowly said, "Yes, Andrew, I still believe in God, but my faith in myself has been shaken."

Andrew responded wisely, "That might be good thing, no?"

As Andrew and I spent time together that summer, I found myself listening more and talking less, and because of that I was amazed at what I learned about him. I discovered that Andrew had been a lawyer in Poland and that he couldn't practice law in the U.S. because he didn't have the money or time to go back to school. I discovered that Andrew had a wife of twenty years named Eva, and two children. I also found out that Andrew was a brilliant man who spoke four languages, studied philosophy, and had a fanatical interest in soccer. As Andrew talked and I listened, he initiated profound spiritual conversations and asked probing questions for which I had few answers.

Over time, the more we walked around the grounds, cutting the lawn and working on the building, the more ashamed I became of my behavior the previous summer. I was afraid that I had single-handedly turned Andrew off to spiritual matters completely. Fortunately that didn't seem to be true; the more Andrew watched me struggle and the more I was honest about what I was feeling, the more spiritual interest he showed. There was something very authentic and natural about the way our relationship unfolded each day.

I began to realize that maybe God was using the contrast between the jerk of the summer before and the newer me. Maybe God was taking my mistake and using it for his purposes as well. I used to think that God could use only our strengths and victories for his glory. Maybe he uses our sins and weaknesses as well.

Which makes me wonder what sin you keep beating yourself up about. As you think about what you did, the stupidity of it, the way in which those you hurt were changed by your actions—as bad as all of that was, maybe it wasn't the final word in the situation. Maybe there's something greater than your sin. Maybe the person staring back at you in the mirror is worth giving another chance after all.

On my last day on the maintenance crew, something happened that will always hold a special place in my heart. After I said goodbye to everyone on my team, Andrew followed me out to my car. He placed both hands on my shoulders and said something I will never forget: "I will miss you, Brian Jones, my friend."

11

SHEPHERDS

Spirituality is not a formula; it is not a test. It is a relationship.
Spirituality is not about competency; it is about intimacy.
Spirituality is not about perfection; it is about connection.
The way of the spiritual life begins where we are now in the
mess of our lives.

—MICHAEL YACONELLI

Let me ask you a very pointed question: who knows the true condition of your soul right now? Would I be correct if I guessed no one? That's got to change. It's rare to find people who finally got rid of the gorilla who didn't also grant someone else access to the interior parts of their souls and allow themselves to be guided to hope and healing. If you struggle with an unforgiving heart and you are ever going to find your way, you need to step out, take a risk, and find a spiritual shepherd to help you learn how to forgive.

In the Bible God makes it clear that people in churches are to be led by those who have the proven ability to lead their congregation into Christlike spiritual maturity. The Bible uses a number of words synonymously to describe these spiritual leaders: *elder, pastor, overseer*, and *shepherd*. While the exact titles vary from book to book of the Bible, the purpose of the role always stays the same: to provide spiritual oversight for everyone in the congregation (1 Peter 5:2).

In the early church, each congregation was charged with installing multiple spiritual shepherds (Philippians 1:1; Titus 1:5). Some were paid while most were not (1 Timothy 5:17, 18). Only those who had first distinguished themselves as having learned how to obey Jesus' teachings were placed into these strenuous but rewarding roles (1 Timothy 3:1-10). These shepherds were meant to be examples to the flock and ultimately held accountable by God for how they spiritually nurtured those entrusted to their care (1 Peter 5:1-4). Shepherds were tasked with protecting the flock from harmful spiritual leaders and influences (Acts 20:28-31) and gently teaching each person in the church how to be formed into a maturing follower of Jesus (Ephesians 4:11-16).

One of the most important things you can do to get rid of the gorilla is place yourself under the care of a spiritual shepherd. God has placed some in your church body for this very purpose. Your shepherd doesn't have to be the senior pastor of a church or even a paid staff member. In fact, because of the level of intimacy that must be developed and the time involved, there are probably far better choices. Any spiritually mature Christ follower could help you in this task. Just look for someone you trust, someone you know will take your secrets to the grave.

In his spiritual classic *Introduction to the Devout Life*, St. Francis de Sales asked men who desired to enter the monastic life, "Do you seriously wish to travel the road to devotion? If so, look for a good man to guide and lead you. This is the most important of all words of advice."[1] (I would encourage women to look for a good woman to guide you.) This is what disciples have done for the past two thousand years.

Here are two ways you can allow a spiritual shepherd to guide you toward a forgiving heart.

LET YOUR SHEPHERD SEE INTO YOUR MESS

I've had my fair share of strange jobs. Going through graduate school I picked weeds for a reclusive German heiress. It paid well, about twenty dollars an hour, but it was stressful. Every twenty minutes the heiress came out and yelled, "Youz doing itz all wrongz!" The hardest job I ever had was working for a construction company during the summer of my sophomore year in college. I never really built anything, though. I mainly lugged around fifty-pound blocks of concrete while the year-round guys slept in the truck. By far my grossest job ever was driving a truck for the General Diaper Delivery Service one sweltering summer break. This was back in the days when women used real diapers and babies expelled unusually large amounts of waste. I'm still in therapy over that job.

None of my jobs, however, compare to the strange jobs photographed by author/photographer Nancy Rica Schiff in her book *Odd Jobs: Portraits of Unusual Occupations*. One day Schiff came across a person with an unusual job—the official timekeeper at a horse race track. She then started wondering about other unusual jobs and set out to photograph the people who do them. Here are a few jobs she photographed that you might not want to apply for:

Occularist. A person who paints fake eyeballs.

Crack filler. Schiff stood on top of Mt. Rushmore and photographed a crack filler repairing Jefferson's nose.

Assistant to knife thrower. How much does that person make?

Bull inseminator. And you think your job is bad?

Porta-potty serviceman. Ever wonder about that guy?

Armpit sniffer. Works for companies that make deodorant.

My personal favorite in Schiff's book is the professional page turner, Louis Yelnick, who turns the pages for famous pianists that accompany other instrumentalists in Carnegie Hall. Yelnick describes himself as "the man behind the man behind the man."[2]

The toughest job I've ever had, something more excruciating and time-consuming than anything Schiff photographed, has been serving as a spiritual shepherd for those inside and outside my congregation. When the biblical writers wanted to find a word to capture the essence of what real Christian community looks like, they used the Greek word *koinonia*, which means "common."[3] It was a word used to describe the way people shared cups and dishes with one another at a meal. When we read in Acts 2:42 that the earliest Christians "devoted themselves to . . . the fellowship [*koinonia*]," we tend to picture people standing around talking before church with a donut in one hand and a cup of coffee in the other. That bears no resemblance to what the biblical writers were describing. *Koinonia* has more in common with the floor of a truck stop restroom than nice happy people shaking hands in a church foyer. *Koinonia* is a word that describes dirt and filth, the closest the biblical writers could come to describing the way the earliest Christians let each other see into the messiness of their lives.

Your shepherd needs to know everything—the pretty and not so pretty. That memory, that piece of your past that you just can't let go, you need to share that with a person you trust who is serving as a shepherd for your soul. That sin you can't bear to tell anyone about? Share that as well. Let this trusted person into the *koinonia* of your life. Give him or her full access to uncover why you keep holding onto your grudge. Grant a free pass to ask any questions and probe anywhere the Spirit leads. This will take a tremendous amount of courage on your part, but it's absolutely necessary. In *Introduction to the Devout Life*, Francis de Sales also wrote, "Open wide your heart so that you can cast out your sins in confession. . . . Be sure to state everything with candor and sincerity and in this way put your conscience completely at rest. This done, listen to the advice and commands of God's minister and say within your heart, 'Speak, Lord, for your servant hears.'"[4]

The Bible says in James 5:14-16, "Is any one of you sick? He should call the elders of the church to pray over him and anoint him with oil in the name of the Lord. And the prayer offered in faith will make the sick person well; the Lord will raise him up." Healing, whether physical or emotional, is not dependent upon the power of an elder's prayer. It's not even dependent upon the confession of a person's sin, even though James continues, "If he has sinned, he will be forgiven. Therefore confess your sins to each other and pray for each other so that you may be healed." Healing occurs when God in his sovereignty chooses to move. It just so happens that the most potent context for a God sighting is smack in the middle of the spiritual triangle of a hurting heart, a loving spiritual shepherd, and the presence of God. That all begins with you and your willingness to open up.

LET YOUR SHEPHERD
TELL YOU THE TRUTH

There's a reason your shepherd needs to know everything: he or she is trying to listen to God on your behalf. With one ear pointed toward your struggle and the other toward heaven, your shepherd's task is to help you understand what God is saying in your situation. Give him or her permission to tell you the truth.

Years ago a spiritual shepherd of mine told me that we each have four rooms in our lives, to which only certain people have the keys.

What we both know. The first room in your life holds what we both know about you. We both hold the keys to this room. It's the surface stuff—I'm six foot two, I am a male, and I like coaching soccer. These are things anyone can easily discover about me.

What you know that I don't know. The second room in your life holds the information that none of us feels comfortable sharing, what you struggle with and are ashamed of, your sins, addictions, and failures. This is the area of life that you keep hidden from other people's view. You're the only one who holds the keys to this room.

What I know about you that you don't know. The third room in your life holds realities about yourself that you are blind to. Just as drivers have blind spots where they cannot see a car in the other lane without turning to look, you have areas in your life that you can't see without additional input. Other people hold the keys to this room, not you.

What only God knows. Finally, the fourth room in your life contains certain things about your life that only God has knowledge about. Only he knows how he feels about you right this second or what is in store for your life. God holds the keys to this room.

Here's the problem: ninety-five percent of the people I've met never have an opportunity to get at the root of what is causing them to harbor an unforgiving heart because they never allow someone else to tell them what's in the third room. Your inability to forgive might be utterly ridiculous, but how will you know if you've never shared the full story with anyone and listened to what he or she had to say in return? Or are you taking too much responsibility for what happened? How will you know if you've never allowed anyone to get to know the real you and speak truth into your life? The Greek word for *truth* comes from *aleitheia*, the combination of *letho*, which means "forgetfulness," and *a*, which means "not."[5] Shepherds don't allow things to escape your notice. Ephesians 4:15 says, "Speaking the truth in love, we will in all things grow up into him who is the Head, that is, Christ." Who is doing the truth speaking? The context makes it clear that it is the spiritual leaders inside the church. Truth speaking can only occur when there is active truth listening.

I have a friend who never was able to get past the pain her uncle caused her by sexually molesting her in her teens. For years she felt that because she somewhat enjoyed the clitoral stimulation that she actually condoned what he did to her. Then a wise spiritual shepherd opened up that third room in her life and pointed out that what she experienced was a simple biological response; it didn't condone what her uncle did in the least. She hadn't led him on or teased him in any way. This one piece of information took a massive load of guilt off her shoulders and pointed her toward forgiveness.

What kills me is the way every person I know who struggles with getting rid of the gorilla pushes away the very people who could help the most. I know it's hard to trust after you've been wounded, *but you must.* You simply must find someone you can trust enough to be a shepherd for you and allow him or her to speak truth into your life.

BETTER THAN ADT

Next to my bed sits a heavy golf club, a Kmart blue-light special pitching wedge to be exact. It cost twelve dollars. Since I no longer own a gun, I keep it there in case someone breaks into my house and I need to pull a ninja jujitsu samurai sort of thing on him. "I pity the fool," as Mr. T used to say, who breaks into my house.

However, I don't usually lie awake at night worrying about intruders. Our neighborhood is pretty safe. And if something arises that my trusty club can't handle, then certainly ADT will do the trick. What I really fear are the things I can't protect myself or my family against. This week two close family members are undergoing second tests for cancer. Another has been without a paycheck for months. Another has been struggling with depression. These are the things that really scare me.

It's recorded very early in the Bible that God came to a man named Abram, who was later called Abraham, and gave him a special promise. The depths of comfort this promise brought to Abram, who was living in a dangerous land at the time, cannot be exaggerated. In Genesis 15:1, God told Abram, "Do not be afraid, Abram. I am your shield."

People don't use shields too much anymore. We see them mostly in museums. But in Abram's time, people knew how vital a good shield was. When arrows and spears rained down on an army like hail, a shield was the only thing that stood between seeing loved ones again and a burial plot.

To know that God is our shield, that he protects us, that he stands in the gap between us and what keeps us awake at night, comforts me immensely. It gives me strength to know that the God of the universe surrounds me, not some piece of wood or steel, especially when it comes to this business of trusting someone enough to share what's really going on in my life and giving him the ability to tell me what he truthfully thinks.

I want you to try something. Remove Abram's name from Genesis 15:1 and insert yours.

"Do not be afraid, _____[insert your name]. I am your shield."

How does that sound? Repeat it over and over again until you start to believe it. "Do not be afraid," God says. "I am your shield. I've got your back." That's God's promise to you.

God's protection makes me think of Saint Patrick. Many think Patrick was a mythical little green guy who made green beer and started St. Paddy's Day. But Patrick not only existed, he was one of the greatest spiritual shepherds of all time. Pirates stole Patrick as a young boy from his home in Roman Britain and took him to Ireland as a slave. There he was cruelly treated until he escaped. Ironically, as a Christian, Patrick felt called to go back to Ireland to introduce people there to Jesus. Patrick's mission to Ireland was wildly successful, but he and his followers faced imminent danger at every turn.

Closing this chapter is a section of a poem known as "Patrick's Lorica," which Patrick's brave spiritual descendants recited in the morning as they faced another day. *Lorica* is Latin for *breastplate*.

Some time ago, I got into the habit of pulling this prayer out at the beginning of every week and praying it out loud. Its words strengthen my heart and embolden my faith. May it do the same for you as you seek to let a spiritual shepherd close enough to help you get rid of the gorilla.

> I arise today
>> with God's strength to pilot me:
>> God's might to uphold me
>> God's wisdom to guide me
>> God's eye to look ahead for me
>> God's ear to hear for me
>> God's word to speak for me
>> God's hand to defend me
>> God's way to lie before me
>> God's shield to protect me
>> God's host to safeguard me.

> ....

>> Christ ever with me, Christ before me, Christ
>>> behind me
>> Christ within me, Christ beneath me, Christ
>>> above me
>> Christ to my right side, Christ to my left
>> Christ in his breadth, Christ in his length, Christ
>>> in depth
>> Christ in the heart of every man who thinks of me
>> Christ in the mouth of every man who speaks to me

Christ in every eye that sees me
Christ in every ear that hears me.

. . . .

Salvation is from the Lord.[6]

12

JOY

With all things, it is always what comes to us from outside,
freely and by surprise, as a gift from heaven, without our
having sought it, that brings us pure joy.

—SIMONE WEIL

I want to conclude our journey together by doing something that might seem a bit odd. I want us to think about why we can be thankful that God has allowed us to be emotionally wrecked and forced to go through the process of forgiving those who have hurt us. My reason is simple: everyone talks about the negative aspects of a wounded heart, but few seek God's perspective on the positives he's trying to accomplish through their turmoil as well. Ironically, it wasn't until I was able to see the really good stuff that came as a result of my struggle to forgive that I began to find the strength to actually do so.

CULTIVATING JOY

A number of years ago, my family and I were sitting inside a Boeing 737 on the runway of Philadelphia International Airport, waiting for our plane to take us to Orlando for a vacation. The roar of the engines seemed to match the emotional turbulence blasting in my head. Just hours earlier I had met for over an hour with an extremely negative person and listened as she informed me that she was leaving our church. Personally, I was overjoyed at her news. Her petty spirit affected just about everyone she came in contact with. I viewed her departure as a blessed subtraction for our church, but I was angry with her negative comments about me.

Pressed for time, I zipped home after the meeting concluded to pick up Lisa and the girls and head for the airport. The excitement in the car was palpable. The prospect of spending time at Disney, going to the beach, doing nothing for an entire week—it was just about all everyone could handle, except me. I was sullen and consumed with the negative comments I had heard just hours before.

On the plane, as I sat in my aisle seat, Lisa to my left and our three girls across the aisle to my right, my entire demeanor screamed anything but vacation. I remember glancing over at Chandler as she tried to make me laugh by sticking her tongue out at me, but I gave her only a polite half smile in return. Five minutes went by, and we were still number twelve in line. Ten minutes went by, and we hadn't budged. Twenty-five more minutes and the captain finally came on the loudspeaker and told us to prepare for takeoff.

Looking straight ahead, unable to shake the mean and malicious comments I had heard at my meeting, I sat focused inward and brooding. Then Lisa elbowed me and told me to look over at the girls. All three had their hands in the air as if they were riding a roller-coaster. Smiling and giggling loud enough to be heard throughout the cabin, they yelled across the aisle for me to join them. "Come on, Dad!"

I hesitated for a moment, and then said, "What the heck!" and threw my hands in the air as we tore off down the runway. The people behind us began to laugh as the plane's front wheels lifted off the ground and all three girls, unrehearsed and full of joy, shouted "Wheeew!!!" at the top of their lungs. I joined them by shouting "Oh yeah baby!" as the back wheels lifted off the ground and we were catapulted into the air. A few seconds later we put our hands down and laughed at the tradition we had started. On every flight since, regardless of where we're seated or where we're going, we always raise our hands like a group of nut balls riding a really scary roller coaster.

Sometimes, regardless of what happens to us in life, we just have to say "What the heck!" and allow ourselves to enjoy this one-and-only life we've been given. Our problems may remain unfixed. Our relationships may remain strained. In our minds our lives may have been unalterably set off course by mean-spirited people. But there comes a time when we have to say, "Life is passing me by while I'm consumed with sadness, bitterness, and negativity. What the heck! I'm going to choose to be joyful, regardless. I'm just going to choose it. I'm going to force myself to choose joy, today, this minute, right now, regardless."

I'm fairly certain that neither of us wants someone to read Mary Oliver's poem "A Bitterness" as the eulogy at our funerals:

I believe you did not have a happy life.

I believe you were cheated.

I believe your best friends were loneliness and misery.

I believe your busiest enemies were anger and depression.

I believe joy was a game you could never play without stumbling.

I believe comfort, though you craved it, was forever a stranger.

I believe music had to be melancholy or not at all.

I believe no trinket, no precious metal, shone so bright as
    your bitterness.

I believe you lay down at last in your coffin none the wiser and
    unassuaged.

Oh, cold and dreamless under the wild, amoral, reckless, peaceful
    flowers of the hillsides.[1]

Struggling with an unforgiving heart, while one of the key reasons I became pessimistic and negative about life, was also the reason I've found myself ultimately able to choose joy. It is as if the struggle has forced me to choose between two extremes—radical pessimism and radical joy. Pessimism is ultimately a dead end, so a few years ago I began choosing joy. I don't know how to put it any differently than that. I just began choosing it. I began forcing myself to fight my natural tendency to look for the negative in people and instead began searching for the positive. It's a habit that I'm still cultivating, with limited success, but it's a habit I know I would not ever have chosen if I had not been forced to choose. Oddly enough, struggling with forgiveness has taught me the spiritual discipline of joy.

NURTURING HUMILITY

There's one verse in the Bible that always makes me laugh. It's found in the Old Testament in the book of Numbers. Strange name for a book, I realize, but it's in there. Numbers 12:3 reads, "Now Moses was a very humble man, more humble than anyone else on the face of the earth." Two things about that verse make me grin. First, how did the person who wrote Numbers find out that Moses was "more humble than anyone else on the face of the earth"? That's quite a statement. Maybe there was a worldwide humility contest the writer knew about but didn't include in the book.

Think about it. Maybe each country held its own national humility qualifying rounds; then sent its winner to the International Humility Olympics held every year in Greece. We probably didn't hear about it because the people who attended were too humble to record their accomplishments for posterity. Contenders probably competed in events like facial expression, receiving compliments, dress, self-deprecating humor, and most important, groveling. Since the book of Numbers claims Moses was the undisputed humility champ of the planet, my hunch is he took gold every year. You can't get much more humble than that.

The other thing that seems comical about this verse is that many Bible scholars believe Moses wrote the book of Numbers himself! Think about *that* for a moment. The most humble person in the world tells us he is, well, the most humble person in the world. There you have it. I don't know how to resolve this strange dilemma. Some scholars say a later editor inserted the comment. Sounds convincing to me.

Throughout the Bible we are told to "humble ourselves" (1 Peter 5:6) and even to be "completely humble" (Ephesians 4:2). Let your eyes rest on that word *completely* for a while. The Bible tells us not to shoot for 34 percent humility or even 76 percent humility. One hundred percent humility is the goal. Now, if you ask me, that's a pretty ambitious target. Whether it's realistic, I'm not so sure, but I do think it's worth aiming at. Why? Intuitively, I think, we all know it's best to be humble. Who doesn't have an obnoxious friend who thinks he's always one step ahead of the crowd? I can think of a few times, just this week, when some self-promoting words crossed my lips. Pride has a way of releasing a kind of relational stench, if you will. Proud people are just not real fun to be around. I know.

Pride is something I really struggle with. Ever since my oldest daughter was three, I've been coaching my daughters' soccer teams. Recently I signed up to take an intensive two-month course to receive what is called a D license to allow me to coach regional travel teams at the premier level. The United States Soccer Federation offers national licensure for coaches, with E the lowest level, then D, then C, B, and A. Those who get E licenses tend to be thirty pounds overweight, have never played soccer before, and end up in the emergency room hyperventilated after practice. Those who get A licenses have played professionally in Europe, stand roughly three foot nine, run at near-Olympic speed, speak Italian, and end up coaching college teams.

Since I had eight solid years of backyard coaching under my belt, I wasn't about to humiliate myself by starting out with a measly little E license. I decided to skip that and go straight for the D license course. The first day of class, I knew I was in trouble.

"People, this is going to be hands-on training," said the class trainer, "three hours a day, three nights a week, all day Saturday, for two months." I thought, *You've got to be kidding! I thought this was just going to be classroom work!* Into the gymnasium we went, and our sadistic trainer, just arrived in the U.S. from some Eastern European country somewhere, asked for volunteers.

I thought, *I'll volunteer first, make an impression, and get this drill over with.* Seventy-five minutes later, I was in the corner heaving. My T-shirt was completely drenched with sweat. My legs felt like rubber. My arms were hurting, and I thought, *Oh great, don't your arms start hurting before you have a heart attack? I'm going to be the first person to die trying to become a soccer coach!*

The hubris with which I thought I could compete with premier-level coaches is nothing compared to the pride I struggle with every day of my life. Someone once told me that every person has two or three besetting sins that tend to trip us up in life. One of mine is pride. I would never be a contender for the gold at the Humility Olympics.

It comes as no surprise, then, that God has gifted me with a predicament that has caused me to humble myself. Forgiveness—genuine forgiveness—never comes from those who are prideful. Forgiving our enemies requires us to swallow our pride. It causes us to allow people to win a fight. It forces us to choose not to retaliate when we know we could. Certain philosophers have made the point that only weak people forgive, which has, in turn, riled up the faithful to provide a stern response. The reality is the philosophers are correct. Only weak, humbled people can find the way to forgiveness. That's a good thing.

SEEKING TO FILL THE VOID

Black holes, many astronomers believe, are big holes in the universe that act like giant vacuum cleaners, sucking whatever gets close enough into their immense gravitational field—small things like dust, meteors, and household pets, as well as large things like planets and stars. The gravitational pull of a black hole is so powerful it even sucks in light. Black holes begin as giant stars that eventually lose their fuel and collapse, imploding so fast and so hard they create something like an inny belly button in time and space. To describe this process astronomers use big words I have to look up, so it helps me to picture a basketball losing air so fast and collapsing so hard under its own weight that it turns into a vacuum cleaner hose. That's the black hole theory in a nutshell.

No one knows exactly where the dust and planets and stars that enter a black hole eventually go. Most astronomers believe they travel through "worm holes" and empty out on the other side of the universe somewhere. My best guess is that it all gets dumped in New Jersey, but this theory hasn't gained widespread acceptance among astronomers yet.

To me, the soul of someone far from God is like a newly formed black hole—large and consuming. It's as if the human soul has a gravitational thirst of its own. We know we are empty, so we try to consume whatever comes into close range in a futile attempt to fill our souls. Some people try to fill their souls with acceptable things like education or a career or kids or a two-car garage in the suburbs. Others try to fill it with alcohol or drugs or sex or fame. Whatever the fix, that's all it turns out to be, just a temporary fix. Nothing ever actually fills the void.

What makes matters worse—or better, depending on how you look at it—is that God recognizes our emptiness and does something to make us even emptier—he sends trials into our lives. To the empty soul God sends things like diabetes and corporate downsizing and marital disharmony. With each trial the black holes in our souls widen and grow and swirl with even more foment and agitation. Eventually we're throwing Jupiter-sized fixes at the black holes yet they remain unfazed, and God smiles, because it is all part of his plan. God knows that at some point we'll figure out that the void can't be filled with anything from this world, and then we'll start looking somewhere else.

Trials and hardships that come from struggling with an unforgiving heart are like large stars that go into the black hole and expand its emptiness. Astronomers believe that the entrance to some black holes expands to ten thousand times the size of our own sun. That's what my soul felt like before I was introduced to Jesus. Each time God allowed hardships in my path, it was as if my void grew. When I wasn't a Christian, there was emptiness at the core of who I was; I could feel it, a mixture of loneliness and fear. With each painful trial, the hole grew larger.

Someone far from God thinks that the void he or she feels is proof of God's absence. My experience has been the exact opposite. The more I struggled with the pain of unforgiveness, the more I sought to alleviate the pain. I just kept looking for something large enough to fill the void until I ran out of places to look. It seems odd to say this, but the gorilla was one of the reasons I stumbled back toward God. As Quaker William Penn said in his classic book *Some Fruits of Solitude*, "We are apt to call things by wrong Names. We will have Prosperity to be Happiness, and Adversity to be Misery; though that is the School of Wisdom, and often-times the way to Eternal Happiness."[2]

HEARING THE MASTER'S VOICE

I brush my teeth and floss two times a day. I like keeping my teeth clean. However, I'm really, really cheap, so I ran a decade-long stretch without going to the dentist. A few years ago, I finally ended the run. The dentist found no cavities, just as I predicted, but he did find enough plaque to fill a small swimming pool. With a wire plaque-picking utensil, he pulled and yanked in places I didn't know existed. After twenty minutes of scraping and maneuvering, he put down his instrument and said in a sweat, "Got it."

The dental assistant put the water hose in my mouth, told me to gargle and spit, and then said, "You're done." The first thing I did was run my tongue along the back of my teeth. *They feel so jagged*, I thought. Ten years of plaque built up along the inside base of my teeth had created one continuous smooth ridge, but the dentist had exposed the natural line of my teeth.

I've been going back over the teachings of Jesus recently. As I grew up in pseudo-Christian culture, the teachings of Jesus had gradually lost their grit and ability to offend me. They had recessed into the amalgam of Scripture, becoming safe, easy, and explainable. I grew accustomed to staring at one of Jesus' teachings, praying, and going about my day. Jesus had no edge to him.

Then I began struggling to get rid of the gorilla, and I began to hear the harshness of Jesus' command to forgive. As I railed against it, I began to hear the fresh voice of Jesus again. I began to under-stand why people walked away from his presence angry and disbe-lieving. "The time has come," Jesus said. "The kingdom of God is near. Repent and believe the good news!" (Mark1:15). I never really felt the brunt of that until I had something I really didn't want to repent of.

A HEART FOR THE POOR

We don't have to read very far in the Gospels to realize that the poor have a special place in the heart of Jesus. In his very first public sermon, Jesus stated that the poor would be a priority in his minis-try: "The Spirit of the Lord is on me, because he has anointed me to proclaim good news to the poor" (Luke 4:18). In Luke's account of the Sermon on the Mount, Jesus' very first words are "Blessed are you who are poor, for yours is the kingdom of God" (Luke 6:20). When John the Baptist was thrown in prison and wondered whether Jesus was actually who he said he was, Jesus sent his friends to John with a message that concluded, "The good news is preached to the poor" (Matthew 11:5). Jesus loved the poor because he was God's Son, but also, I think, because being poor himself he understood their sense of frustration and anxiety as they tried to provide for their daily needs.

It's no wonder Jesus responded the way he did, recorded in Mark 8, when thousands had gathered to listen to his teachings and remained there for three days. I think we can assume that because the people stayed with Jesus for so long, most of them were the poorest of the poor—without jobs, without obligations to tie them down, and without anywhere else to turn for help. I think that as Jesus stared out at this sea of brokenness his lips began to quiver, his jaw began to tighten, his chest became heavy, and his breathing became labored, and I think he choked back tears. Then, turning to his closest followers, he said, "I have compassion for these people; they have already been with me three days and have nothing to eat. If I send them home hungry, they will collapse on the way" (vv. 2, 3).

Have you ever been poor? Are you struggling financially now? For the first two years of our marriage, Lisa and I were broke. We were both finishing school full-time; the small amount of income I generated came from building computers during the week and preaching at a small rural church on the weekends. I'll never forget the time we went to a neighborhood pizza shop for a special occasion. We were starving and barely had enough money to buy a small pizza and water. Next to us sat a table full of police officers eating a culinary feast—pizza, salads, and dessert. When they got up, they left four pieces of pizza on their table, and I looked at Lisa and asked, "Are you thinking what I'm thinking?" She answered, "Absolutely not!" To try to soothe her conscience, I gave her a passionate speech about wasting God's resources and how God would actually be happy if we ate that pizza. She didn't buy it.

When the coast was clear, I gingerly slid the pizza onto our table, and we shoved the pieces into our mouths. Seconds later Lisa looked up and yelled, "Sheezz!" Two police officers were coming back to the table next to us, and one had a to-go box in his hands! With an entire piece of pizza in my mouth, I stared at Lisa and said in a muffled voice, "Game faces, woman. Hold it together. Breathe. Don't crack! I'm not going to the big house over this."

Theologians talk a lot about "Jesus' preferential option for the poor," which is an academic way of saying that God has a huge heart for those who are financially destitute. Do you want to know what's interesting? The more I've wrestled with the painful effects of living with an unforgiving heart in recent years, the more I've felt my heart soften for people in need. It's as if my pain, though caused by a different source, senses a connection with anyone I see in need. I've begun to empathize in a greater way with those God's heart goes out to.

I haven't always felt this strange pull toward those in need. Years ago when we moved to Ohio to start a new church, we soon faced a major obstacle: we had outgrown the school we were renting for Sunday church services. Eventually we located another place to meet, a large space in a shopping center, but the city zoning officials wanted us to make outrageously expensive improvements to the building, and we didn't have the money. In an effort to get the township to drop some of its requirements, I asked the city zoning officer to join me for lunch.

As I waited in my office for my appointment, both the zoning officer and another man named Larry showed up at the same time. Larry was a homeless man who had visited our church the previous Sunday. When the zoning officer asked, "Ready to go to lunch?" Larry smiled and said, "Lunch?" The zoning officer asked, "Pastor, is your parishioner joining us?"

No sooner had I stammered "Uhhhh . . . " than Larry blurted, "I'd love to go."

Larry wasn't exactly the kind of guy I wanted to go with me to broker a deal. He hadn't showered in at least a week. His hair was greasy, he was missing quite a few teeth, he wore a dark blue hand-me-down blazer with torn blue jeans and mismatched high-top basketball shoes, and piles of dandruff lay like coconut shavings on both shoulders. When we sat down at our table, Larry took his right hand and brushed all the dandruff off his shoulders and onto our menus.

I can't believe this is happening, I thought. I was dying inside the entire meal. I remember praying, *Jesus, make this guy go to the bathroom so I can tell the zoning officer he's not a member of our church!* Periodically Larry leaned over and put his finger in my food and said, "You gonna eat that?"

"No, Larry," I would say. "You can have it."

Somehow we eventually we got down to business. As the zoning officer and I discussed our church's dilemma, Larry sat quietly and nodded his head as he slurped his soup. After listening to my impassioned plea to eliminate some of the township's financial constraints, Larry put down his spoon. I could see that he wanted to butt in, and I silently asked God to intervene in some way—a small earthquake, locusts, anything.

No such luck. Larry looked across the table, put his arm around me, and said to the zoning officer, "Jim—can I call you Jim? Do you see Pastor Brian here? Pastor Brian here is the best %$#@ pastor I've ever seen! Have you heard this guy preach? Man, can he preach! Well, here's the deal, Jim. You need to listen real close. Our church needs a building, so I'd suggest you make this little deal happen. You know what I'm talking about, Jim?" Then Larry looked over at me, nodded his head, and winked as if to say "That should take care of it." I thought, *Yep, we're dead.*

When we got back to the church office, I pulled the zoning officer to the side and tried to do damage control. I explained that our church members were hip young professionals and that Larry was a recent homeless visitor, but I could tell by his terse words that his impression of who we were as a church was already formed. I shook his hand, said good-bye, walked right past Larry, and said, "Thanks a lot."

That afternoon as I began writing my sermon, I felt as if God was saying, "Are you a fool? What's more important, a person or a building?" I felt such a mixture of emotions—guilt, embarrassment, anger, and confusion—that I couldn't concentrate any longer; I walked out of my office and called it a day. On the way home I looked at the expensive houses I was passing on my right and left, and I thought of Larry, who at that moment was probably riding the public bus back downtown. Not coincidentally, it wasn't long after this incident that all the emotions of an unforgiving heart began to bubble to the surface.

I haven't treated someone in need like that since.

FINDING PERSPECTIVE

Years ago in a short story called "The Capital of the World," Ernest Hemingway wrote, "Madrid is full of boys named Paco, which is the diminutive of the name Francisco, and . . . a father . . . came to Madrid and inserted an advertisement in the personal columns of *El Liberal* which said: PACO MEET ME AT HOTEL MONTANA NOON TUESDAY. ALL IS FORGIVEN PAPA." So many young men went out to greet their fathers, Hemingway wrote, eight hundred in all, that an entire police squadron had to be deployed to restore civil order.[3]

When I first read that story, I immediately thought of all the pain that exists in families in our world, all the wrecked marriages and abuse that causes good kids to grow up to be mean teenagers who grow into adults who hurt those around them. I thought of all the people I've known who carry pain inflicted by someone who used to be one of those good kids turned mean teenager turned angry adult. And I thought of the young man who forever changed my life on one cold October evening so many years ago, the young man that I wrote about in chapter one who beat me up and laughed at me in court.

A few years ago, Lisa, the girls, and I went back to where I grew up to spend Thanksgiving week with my parents and sisters. The morning after Thanksgiving I got up early and decided to go for a walk. At the corner of Kae Avenue, I went right and headed up the back way behind Rosemore Junior High School. Everything had changed since I was a kid. The homes were all older and seemed much smaller than I remembered them. Thirty minutes into my walk, I came upon the track where I ran the 400-yard dash and threw the discus. Ten minutes later I came to the edge of a park I knew all too well. I hadn't been there since I was in seventh grade.

Not quite sure I wanted to go any further, something inside me told me it would be good to keep on. I walked past the football field where I used to play for the Steelers and where my friend Eric Green and I won the championship in sixth grade. I passed tennis courts that had been turned into a skate park and basketball hoops with nets all ripped away. Finally I came to the corner of the football field where the snack shack used to sit.

The field looked smaller and more run-down than I remembered it. Most of the trees were gone. I glanced to my left and saw where I had stood near the snack shack as a twelve-year-old boy. I pictured the large high school guy standing in front of me, punching me over and over again, and his cronies standing around kicking me in the side. Then I pictured them all slowly walking away when it wasn't fun anymore. I stood there and imagined myself getting up off the ground, bleeding, but my mind quickly turned to the ringleader, laughing as he walked away into the distance.

I pictured him walking back into the low-income houses on the other side of Country Club Road, and opening the door and walking into his house. I stood there and wondered what that home was like for him, and then in my mind I heard a noise. I saw his father emerge from the other room in a drunken stupor and begin hitting him for being too loud; I saw him push his father back in a fit of rage. I began to sense what his life must have been like growing up inside that home. I knew what my friends who grew up in that neighborhood went through; I knew that my imagination on this day was unfortunately very close to reality.

As I stood there, an inescapable sense of sadness came over me. I began to think of my parents and everything I had been given growing up. I thought again of my assailant and began to wonder what his life was like today, if he was married, if he knew how to love his wife, if he had found the love of Christ or not. Then I did something that I had never, ever done before. I said a prayer for him.

I prayed for God to come into his life. I prayed that no matter how dark his childhood was growing up that he'd find the strength to become the man God created him to be. I prayed for his wife. I prayed for his kids. I prayed for him to find joy. I prayed that his kids would grow up to know the love of Jesus. I prayed for him and his family to find a loving church home. The list of things I prayed just flowed from my heart.

Then as I began to walk away, I noticed something. I felt free. For the first time in my life, some twenty-five years after the fact, I had finally forgiven him. I stopped a few hundred yards away and looked back. My eyes started to mist. I smiled and I prayed a simple two-word prayer: "Thank you."

That was the day that I knew I could do it: I knew I could get rid of the gorilla. I'm not there yet, but I'm close.

I'm almost there.

NOTES

CHAPTER ONE, ORIGINS

C. S. Lewis, *Mere Christianity* (1952; New York: HarperSanFrancisco, 2001), 115.

1. Albert Camus, translated by Matthew Ward, *The Stranger* (New York: Vintage Books, 1989), 122.

2. Colin Brown, ed., *The New International Dictionary of New Testament Theology* (Grand Rapids: Zondervan, Regency Reference Library, 1986), 1:697–700.

CHAPTER TWO, RAGE

Gordon MacDonald, as quoted in the introduction by Mark Galli to *Mastering Personal Growth*, by Maxie Dunnam, Gordon MacDonald, and Donald W. McCullough (Sisters: Multnomah, 1992), 11.

1. Colin Brown, ed., *The New International Dictionary of New Testament Theology* (Grand Rapids: Zondervan, Regency Reference Library, 1986), 1:107.

2. Dian Fossey, *Gorillas in the Mist* (New York: Houghton Mifflin, 2000), xv.

3. Ibid., 11, 55, 62–63.

4. Gerhard Kittel and Gerhard Friedrich, eds., translated and abridged in one volume by Geoffrey W. Bromiley, *Theological Dictionary of the New Testament*, (Grand Rapids: William B. Eerdmans, 1985), 339.

5. Frederick Buechner, *Wishful Thinking: A Seeker's ABC*, rev. ed. (New York: HarperSanFrancisco, 1993), 2.

CHAPTER THREE, DISTANCE

James Baldwin, *Notes of a Native Son* (Boston: Beacon Press, 1957), 101.

1. *Webster's New Universal Unabridged Dictionary*, sec. ed. (New York: Simon & Schuster, 1983), 962.

2. John Steinbeck, *Travels with Charley* (New York: Penguin, 2002), 37.

3. Norman Cousins, *Dr. Schweitzer of Lambaréné* (New York: Harper & Brothers, 1960), 220.

4. Eugene O'Neill, *Long Day's Journey into Night*, sec. ed. (New Haven: Yale University Press, 2002), 63.

5. Ibid., 142.

CHAPTER FOUR, PESSIMISM

Watchman Nee, *The Normal Christian Life* (Peabody, Massachusetts: Hendrickson Publishers, 2006), 3.

1. *Webster's New Universal Unabridged Dictionary*, sec. ed. (New York: Simon & Schuster, 1983), 1608.

2. *Beowulf*, translated by Seamus Heaney (New York: W. W. Norton & Company, 2000).

3. Sandra Cisneros, *The House on Mango Street* (New York: Random House, 1991), 11.

4. Thomas Merton, *Thoughts in Solitude* (New York: Farrar, Straus and Giroux, 1958), 49.

CHAPTER FIVE, MYTHS

Dr. David Stoop and Dr. James Masteller, *Forgiving Our Parents, Forgiving Ourselves: Healing Adult Children of Dysfunctional Families* (Ann Arbor: Servant Publications, 1996), 205.

1. St. Augustine, translated by J. B. Shaw, *The Enchiridion on Faith, Hope and Love* (Washington, D. C.: Regnery Publishing, 1996), 87.

2. *The Large Catechism of Martin Luther*, translated by Robert H. Fischer (Philadelphia: Fortress Press, 1959), 77.

3. John Calvin, translated by A. W. Morrison, *Matthew, Mark, and Luke: A Harmony of the Gospels*, (Grand Rapids: Eerdmans, 1980), 1:214.

4. Jonathan Edwards, *The Religious Affections* (Carlisle: Banner of Truth Trust, 1986), 281.

CHAPTER SIX, BELIAL

C. S. Lewis, *The Screwtape Letters* (1942; New York: HarperCollins, 2001), ix.

1. Shakespeare, *Hamlet*, in *The Complete Works of William Shakespeare: The Cambridge Text* (London: Octopus Books, 1980), act 5, scene 2, 919.

2. *The Divine Comedy of Dante Alighieri: Inferno*, translated by Allen Mandelbaum (New York: Bantam Dell, 2004), 301.

CHAPTER SEVEN, CALL

Juan Carlos Ortiz, *Disciple* (Altamonte Springs: Strang, 1975), 31.

1. The three places where the word *Christian* is found in the Bible are Acts 11:26, Acts 26:28, and 1 Peter 4:16.

2. Ben Witherington, III, *The Acts of the Apostles: A Socio-Rhetorical Commentary* (Grand Rapids: Eerdmans, 1998), 371.

3. Dallas Willard, *The Spirit of the Disciplines: Understanding How God Changes Lives* (New York: HarperCollins, 1988), 258.

4. Colin Brown, ed., *The New International Dictionary of New Testament Theology* (Grand Rapids: Zondervan, Regency Reference Library, 1986), 1:483.

5. Willard, *Spirit of the Disciplines*, 263.

6. Brown, *New International Dictionary of New Testament Theology*, 1:144.

CHAPTER EIGHT, KINDNESS

Lewis B. Smedes, *Forgive & Forget: Healing the Hurts We Don't Deserve* (New York: Simon & Schuster, 1986), 137.

1. James Baldwin, *Notes of a Native Son* (Boston: Beacon Press, 1957), 29.

2. W. Somerset Maugham, *Of Human Bondage*, (1915; New York: Bantam, 1991), 331.

3. Oswald Chambers, *My Utmost for His Highest* (New York: Dodd, Mead & Company, 1963), 235.

4. Thomas à Kempis, translated by Leo Sherley-Price, *The Imitation of Christ* (New York: Penguin, 1952), 29.

CHAPTER NINE, PRAYER

H. Norman Wright, *Always Daddy's Girl* (Ventura: Gospel Light, 2001), 235–236.

1. Joseph Katz, ed., *The Complete Poems of Stephen Crane* (Ithaca: Cornell University Press, 1972), 70.

2. Ralph P. Martin, *The Epistle of Paul to the Philippians: An Introduction and Commentary* (Grand Rapids: Eerdmans, 1983), 169.

3. Gerald F. Hawthorne, *Word Biblical Commentary, Philippians* (Waco: Word, 1983), 184–185.

4. Janet Whitney, ed., *The Journal of John Woolman* (Chicago: Henry Regnery Company, 1950), 132.

5. Owen Chadwick, ed., *Western Asceticism* (Philadelphia: Westminster Press, 1958), 51.

CHAPTER TEN, MIRROR

George MacDonald, *Unspoken Sermons* (Charleston, South Carolina: BiblioBazaar, 2006), 46–47.

1. A. Kent Hieatt and Constance Hieatt, eds., *The Canterbury Tales by Geoffrey Chaucer* (New York: Bantam, 1964), lines 537–543.

2. John Bunyan, *The Pilgrim's Progress* (Grand Rapids: Zondervan, 1967), 40.

3. Oswald Chambers, *My Utmost for His Highest* (New York: Dodd, Mead & Company, 1963), 204.

4. Blaise Pascal, *Pensées*, translated by A. J. Krailsheimer (New York: Penguin, 1995), 285.

CHAPTER ELEVEN, SHEPHERDS

Michael Yaconelli, *Messy Spirituality: God's Annoying Love for Imperfect People* (Grand Rapids: Zondervan, 2002), 13.

1. St. Francis de Sales, translated by John K. Ryan, *Introduction to the Devout Life* (New York: Doubleday, 1989), 45.

2. Nancy Rica Schiff, *Odd Jobs: Portraits of Unusual Occupations* (Berkeley: Ten Speed Press, 2002), 4.

3. Colin Brown, ed., *The New International Dictionary of New Testament Theology* (Grand Rapids: Zondervan, Regency Reference Library, 1986), 1:639.

4. de Sales, 71–72.

5. *Liddell and Scott's Greek-English Lexicon*, abridged (Oxford: Clarendon Press, 1989), 32, 411.

6. *The Confession of St. Patrick*, translated by John Skinner, (New York: Doubleday, 1998), 79–81.

CHAPTER TWELVE, JOY

Simone Weil, translated by Arthur Wills, *Gravity and Grace* (New York: G. P. Putnam's Sons, 1952), 94.

1. Mary Oliver, *New and Selected Poems*, (Boston: Beacon Press, 1992), 1:43.

2. William Penn, *Some Fruits of Solitude* (1693; Richmond, Indiana: First Friends United Press, 1978), p. 39.

3. Ernest Hemingway, *The Short Stories* (New York: Scribner, 2003), 38.

ACKNOWLEDGMENTS

When I finished my first book, I thought I'd never write another one, so I thanked everyone from Jesus to my electrician. I'll try to keep this short and sweet.

Diane Stortz—Thanks for working your editing magic on this book. To see other books Diane has edited, go to www.izzysoffice.com.

The Standard team—It's been a pleasure working on another book with you.

CCV staff—We have the greatest staff team anywhere. Thanks for granting me the privilege of serving God through writing.

John Samples—Thanks for taking me out to Pizza Hut in Grayson so many years ago and telling me, "All great preachers have one thing in common. They all know how to tell a story."

Uncle Ron—As promised. Thanks for the great memories growing up, especially for the week fishing with Jeff in Michigan. Thanks for marrying way out of your league. By the way, I'm still waiting on those football cards you owe me.

Mom—Thanks for signing me up for football in first grade when Dad thought I'd get hurt. Thanks for the way you take care of Grandma and Lyn. Thanks for loving my kids like they were your own.

Dad—Thanks for making us stop at boring Civil War battlefields when we were kids. Thanks for breakfasts on Saturday mornings after my high school football games. Thanks for showing me what a Christian man looks like.

Sher—Thanks for beating up Les Setzer for me in the fourth grade. Thanks for being a great mom to Gabrielle and Jeremy. Thanks for always getting all the families together.

Laura—Thanks for loving animals while we grew up as kids, all fifty bazillion of them. Thanks for being a great mom to Megan and Cole. Thanks for staying close to Mom and Dad.

Kelsey, Chandler, and Cammy—Thanks for telling me when I dress like a dork. Thanks for making your faith your own even though I'm a pastor. Thanks for letting me coach your sports teams. Thanks for being the joy of my life.

Lisa—Thanks for your smile. Thanks for the way you love our daughters. Thanks for giving up your career to move to Philly to start a new church. Thanks for introducing me to melted peanut butter and chocolate swirled together and eaten with a spoon. Thanks for the day we spent in Lahaina eating at Cheeseburger in Paradise. Thanks for being my world.

For information about the author's writing, visit his website, www.brianjones.com.

AN EXCERPT FROM

Second Guessing God

hanging on

when you can't

see his plan

BRIAN JONES

WHERE'S GOD?

The Bible tells us that for over four hundred years God's people were slaves in Egypt, until God raised up Moses to lead them out of bondage. After their miraculous escape, God did not instruct the people to build a city immediately outside the borders of Egypt. Instead, he told them to follow as he led them to the land he had promised centuries ago to their forefather Abraham, a place of abundance, flowing with milk and honey.

Because of their disobedience, however, a journey that should have taken a month or so eventually took forty years. Now those who were children when they escaped Egypt stood with *their* children and viewed the promised land with their own eyes. They could hardly contain their excitement. Joshua 3 picks up the story: "Early in the morning Joshua and all the Israelites set out from Shittim and went to the Jordan, where they camped before crossing over" (v. 1).

Picture a massive gathering of people, the kind of assembly you see only at political conventions or rock concerts. Over a million people had waited their entire adult lives for this moment. All that stood between them and their future home was the Jordan River. Imagine the excitement as Joshua gave the people God's instructions about when they were to cross the Jordan into the promised land. "When you see the ark of the covenant of the LORD your God, and the priests, who are Levites, carrying it, you are to move out from your positions and follow it. Then you will know which way to go, since you have never been this way before" (vv. 3, 4).

The Israelites soon discovered that Joshua left out one tiny but important detail in his instructions. Joshua 3:15 tells us that the Jordan is at *flood* stage all during harvest. What time of the year was it? You guessed it—*harvest* season! At any other time of year, God's people could have waded across the Jordan, but not during the floods of the harvest season. The river had turned into a raging deluge.

To realize how frightening it must have appeared, you need to understand the topography of the Jordan River valley. On maps the area looks like a roller coaster. One scholar calls it "the earth's deepest valley."[4] The Jordan River begins at the Sea of Galilee and travels just over sixty miles south, where it empties into the Dead Sea, the lowest place on the planet, thirteen hundred feet below sea level. Most of the year it is a tranquil, meandering river, but during harvest season the rainwater converges in the valley basin, and it becomes a swollen torrent.

FACING THE IMPOSSIBLE

We can only imagine how terrifying the Jordan must have looked to mothers holding the hands of their tiny children or to elderly couples clinging to each other. Those with disabilities, those who were sick or blind must have wiped the mist off their faces with panic. Even the swift and strong among the Israelites must have wondered why God had brought them to this point only to let them die. But the passage continues, "Yet as soon as the priests who carried the ark reached the Jordan and their feet touched the water's edge, the water from upstream stopped flowing. It piled up in a heap a great distance away, at a town called Adam" (vv. 15, 16).

Did you catch that? *As soon as the priests' feet touched the water,* God caused the water to stop flowing. In fact, the Bible later tells us that the water stopped completely, the riverbed dried up, and God's people were able to cross over on dry ground. Where did God stop the flow of water? Did it stop right where the people were standing? Did the Israelites see God at work with their own eyes? No. The water "piled up in a heap a great distance away, at a town called Adam" (v. 16).

Scholars estimate the town of Adam was roughly nineteen miles upstream from where the Israelites stood, far beyond where they could see. It was a miracle, but it was a miracle the people didn't witness with their own eyes. God performed the miracle upstream, out of their sight.

I believe the same situation occurs in our lives today. Here's the powerful truth the children of Israel learned that day: *God is always at work upstream in our lives.*

Where's God? Whenever we face a problem in our lives— sickness, job loss, depression, tragedy, or discouragement—God is at work *upstream* in those situations, beyond our line of sight. The only thing the Israelites could see was the problem right in front of them. They could have concluded that since that raging river was there, God wasn't actively involved in their situation, but they would have been wrong. He was there; they just couldn't see him at work.[5]

GOD IS ALWAYS AT WORK UPSTREAM

When I think of examples of God working upstream, I immediately think of the story of my wife, Lisa, who was given up for adoption at birth. Her adoptive parents were Christians and seemed to have a solid marriage when they adopted her, but over the years they realized that even a child couldn't fix their individual wounds. Their relationship grew apart, and their marriage ended in a tumultuous divorce when Lisa was six years old. From that time on Lisa was raised by her mother alone. Times were tremendously difficult for both of them, but they were involved in a loving church that supported them through it all.

Soon after we were married, Lisa expressed interest in finding her biological parents. We couldn't locate them then, but ten years later we resumed the search with the help of the Internet and located both her birth mother and father within one week. To add to the excitement, Lisa learned that she had four half brothers and sisters. Within one month she drove or flew to meet them all.

One of Lisa's half brothers described at length the odd, destructive behavior Lisa's birth mother had engaged in throughout her life. "You're the lucky one," he said. "You escaped." When Lisa heard the whole story, she realized that this was true; she really was the lucky one. Even though, growing up, her life was hard at times, the difficulties were nothing compared to what she would have experienced if her birth mother had kept her. In addition, Lisa's adoptive mother and the church Lisa attended with her had a profound spiritual impact on Lisa's life. This never would have occurred had she stayed with her birth mother. Best of all, Lisa has been given an opportunity to reach out to her newfound family members with the love of Jesus. She hopes now to be a part of what God is doing upstream in *their* lives.

PROVIDENCE

Theologians have a term for God working upstream. They call it the providence of God. Biblical scholar G. W. Bromiley defines *providence* as "the divine governance whereby all possible events are woven into a coherent pattern and all possible developments are shaped to accomplish the divinely instituted goal."[6]

The key part of the word *providence* is the verb *provide*. God is always working behind the scenes in the events of our lives to provide us with something. This is exactly what the apostle Paul said in Romans 8:28: "And we know that in all things God works for the good of those who love him, who have been called according to his purpose."

Notice two things in this verse. First, God works in *all* things; second, he is always working upstream *for our good.* Nothing ever happens to us that doesn't ultimately accomplish God's goals for our lives. God's providence means he is always working behind the scenes, outside of our view, to provide us with *something,* even when we don't understand what's happening at the time.

At the church I serve, I've taught about God working upstream many times, and over the years it has become a mantra among the people in the congregation. I hear it repeated all the time. Something happens to someone—a bad report from the doctor, a child going through hard times, relationship difficulties—and I'll overhear someone else say, "Let me pray for you. God is working upstream in your life right now. Let's pray that he gives you the strength to hold on until you find out what he's doing."

One powerful example of this happened in the life of a dear saint I know named Ruth Ann. (A number of years ago, I attended a Greek Orthodox festival and toured the congregation's beautiful church building. Pointing out the murals on the walls, the tour guide remarked that her pastor once said the reason the Greek Orthodox church has saints is that "saints make it a little bit easier to believe in God." That phrase moved me so much I almost joined their church right on the spot!)

One day Ruth Ann, who was in her late sixties at the time, came down with pneumonia. At two in the morning, she called the ambulance. Ruth Ann was a tough gal, leathered by a hard life, so it didn't surprise me to learn she had asked the paramedics not to use their sirens because she didn't want to wake up her son! The following day I went to see Ruth Ann in the hospital and sat down next to her bed. She was asleep and had an oxygen mask on her face. I reached out and held her hand. She slowly opened her eyes and smiled underneath the mask. I softly said, "You sleep. I'm just here to pray."

A few minutes later Ruth Ann lifted up her mask, just enough so I could hear her whisper, "I know why I'm here. I know why God allowed me to have pneumonia. My nurse is a single mother. She's going through a tough time. I prayed with her last night."

That's God working upstream. More importantly, that's an example of someone who knows the God who is working upstream.

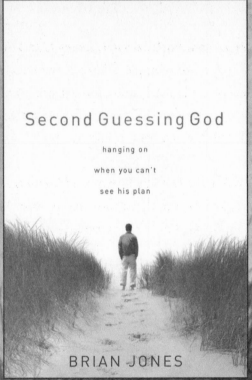

What readers wrote to Brian Jones about his first book,
SECOND GUESSING GOD

Thank you for your book *Second Guessing God*. I'm still not finished with it. I've cried countless times throughout, as it has totally spoken to where I'm at. I'm not "through the woods" yet . . . but maybe for the first time in well over a year, I see the edge. Thanks, Brian, and God bless you in your ministry.

~

Just wanted to tell you how much *Second Guessing God* has helped my wife and me through a very difficult stretch—given us hope and new courage. Thanks for writing!

~

I am just reading *Second Guessing God* for the second time. It has been very helpful for me. I plan to purchase a few more copies to share with friends who are also struggling. Four years ago my brother became a quadriplegic. We have cried out and asked why, and we have begged for a miracle. Your book has helped me to see that we have been given a miracle, the miracle of endurance. We could never have endured this tragedy without God, and I know that he is upstream working things out for us in the end. I just wanted to say what an encouragement your writing has been for me. May God bless and multiply your talents to help others in despair.

~

Thank you for writing *Second Guessing God*. Also, thank you for your honesty. I read it in one night and every page hit me. I highlighted the entire book.

~

I bought six additional copies to help a few friends on their journey to the image of Christ. I really liked the idea of "miracles of perseverance" and your explanation of the apostles' doubt as the great commission was issued. That concept really helped me feel "normal" among all of my doubts, especially as we head off to Bible college.

~

I am in that desert place, and it's so hard to see God's plan. You see, it's not me who is struggling but my son, who was diagnosed with ADHD at age seven. He has struggled most of his life with this disorder, and it has taken a toll on him, my husband and me, and my son's whole social circle. It is the most unbelievable pain to watch this beautiful boy spiral out of control. I turned to your book looking for answers, and I have to say I've found a little more ground to stand on. Thank you so much for your beautiful book. It really has helped me in so many times of great need.

~

Wow! Your book really helped me change my outlook about church and ministry. I was a pastor's kid, and just in the last couple of years my husband became a Christian and then felt a call to the ministry and well, I ran for the hills and nearly lost my faith in the process. Thank you for your book, and I have already passed my copy on and plan on keeping a few on hand to hand out more.

~

I'm a bookseller, and I just finished *Second Guessing God*. Not only will I be hand-selling it and giving it as a gift to every hurting person I know, it has helped me tremendously, and I plan to reread portions, doing some serious application to our family situation. We've never been in such an incredibly dark, lonely, and painful place. Your book touched on so many areas of our pain. Thank you for writing an important book. Thank you for not withholding the gritty realities of pain in this place that is not heaven while helping us hope for that better place.

~

Second Guessing God is an excellent book, very down to earth, that common people can understand and apply. No formulas or 101 steps. No lofty ideals that we all want to aspire to but fail at miserably every day, wondering why we can't "git 'er done" the way the some "good Christians" seem to. You are very honest and transparent. You allowed yourself to be real and shared what so many are thinking (and going through) but never are free to share for fear of judgment and condemnation. This is the best book I have read, on a personal level, in a very long time. This is one of those books that I will buy for others to read. God has gifted you in many ways.

~

I finished your book a couple of days ago. What a blessing— such honest soul searching. I could hardly put it down. Keep it up. Many people should be made to think about life's problems; we sometimes don't want to be honest about them. You make that seem a bit easier—and certainly more satisfying.

~

I just finished reading your book, and I wanted to tell you how much it touched me. I have spent my life wondering where God was in my childhood. I can't see that God did anything to help my situation, and I feel guilty for my doubts about him. I especially appreciated your chapter on mystery. Perhaps now I will honestly express what I am feeling and thinking to God.

~

Your book was so refreshing to me, especially in its openness, candor, and vulnerability. I saw myself frequently in your writing, and it was very comforting and encouraging to me. Thank you so much. You have done a great service for believers who are hurting and feel alone and damaged. I look forward to reading your future books.

~

I've just completed my third reading. I lost track of how many times tears came to my eyes. Brian, your style is comfortable, engaging and, most important, relatable. You truly have a gift.

~

I lost my sixteen-year-old son in an accident a year and a half ago. I read so many books on grieving, and many helped me get through the first year of tremendous anguish. I just finished *Second Guessing God* and tried so hard to read it slowly because I was saying yes, yes with every sentence and wanted to keep rereading the same paragraph all over again! I just couldn't put it down. Without having lost a child yourself, you do understand the dark place of my soul, and you spoke right to my heart. Thank you for your compassion and straightforwardness and for this treasured book that I hold in my hand.

~

I have been feeling like I haven't been hearing from God. I have trouble reading for long periods of time, but I sat for five hours and read the entire book. My wife and I know this was a miracle.

~

Thank you for sharing your story, your pain, and your conclusions about the God who does indeed love us enough to allow us to hurt, bleed, cry, and scream. Please keep writing such edification.